ROUTLEDGE LIBRARY EDITIONS: LITERARY THEORY

Volume 16

DECONSTRUCTION AND THE POLITICS OF CRITICISM

DECONSTRUCTION AND THE POLITICS OF CRITICISM

SIBEL IRZIK

LONDON AND NEW YORK

First published in 1990 by Garland Publishing

This edition first published in 2017
by Routledge
2 Park Square, Milton Park, Abingdon, Oxon OX14 4RN

and by Routledge
711 Third Avenue, New York, NY 10017

Routledge is an imprint of the Taylor & Francis Group, an informa business

© 1990 Sibel Irzik

All rights reserved. No part of this book may be reprinted or reproduced or utilised in any form or by any electronic, mechanical, or other means, now known or hereafter invented, including photocopying and recording, or in any information storage or retrieval system, without permission in writing from the publishers.

Trademark notice: Product or corporate names may be trademarks or registered trademarks, and are used only for identification and explanation without intent to infringe.

British Library Cataloguing in Publication Data
A catalogue record for this book is available from the British Library

ISBN: 978-1-138-69377-7 (Set)
ISBN: 978-1-315-52921-9 (Set) (ebk)
ISBN: 978-1-138-68497-3 (Volume 16) (hbk)
ISBN: 978-1-138-68501-7 (Volume 16) (pbk)
ISBN: 978-1-315-54352-9 (Volume 16) (ebk)

Publisher's Note
The publisher has gone to great lengths to ensure the quality of this reprint but points out that some imperfections in the original copies may be apparent.

Disclaimer
The publisher has made every effort to trace copyright holders and would welcome correspondence from those they have been unable to trace.

DECONSTRUCTION AND THE POLITICS OF CRITICISM

Sibel Irzik

GARLAND PUBLISHING
New York & London
1990

Copyright © 1990 by Sibel Irzik
All Rights Reserved

Library of Congress Cataloging-in-Publication Data

Irzik, Sibel.
Deconstruction and the politics of criticism/ Sibel Irzik.
p. cm.—(Garland studies in comparative literature)
Originally presented as the author's thesis (doctoral) to the Comparative Literature Dept., Indiana University, 1988.
Includes bibliographical references.
ISBN 0-8240-0145-1 (alk. paper)
1. Criticism—Political aspects. 2. Deconstruction. I. Title. II. Series.
PN98.P64I79   1990
801'.095—dc20   90-3642

To my parents

Contents

Preface	ix
Acknowledgments	xi
Chapter 1. Introduction	3
Chapter 2. Deconstructing Ideology	11
Chapter 3. Literature Against Ideology and Metaphysics	37
Chapter 4. Deconstructing the Subject	55
Chapter 5. Criticism and Communities	75
Chapter 6. Conclusion	87
Works Cited	91

Preface

This work was submitted as a doctoral dissertation to the Comparative Literature Department of Indiana University in 1988. Its purpose was to call attention to the contrast between the remarkable politicization of the rhetoric of literary criticism in recent years and the scarcity of interest in the concrete historical and political contexts of literary texts. Deconstruction, with its easily detectable totalizing tendencies and theoreticism, offered a natural target for such a critique. Perhaps more interesting to notice was the similarity which emerged between deconstruction and theories far removed from it when it came to applying the results of general theoretical analyses to the area of literary criticism. Even in the case of the most overtly political formulations, literature seemed to enjoy a certain aloofness from the more or less hostile world of history and social conflicts. Whether this world was the cripplingly deterministic one of ideology or metaphysics, or the disillusioningly arbitrary one of paradigms and communities, literary texts were always one step ahead of the game, either as self-demistifiers or as products of an inscrutable consensus within communities. What started out as a rejection of the New Critical dogma about the special status of literature often led to its reiteration.

The overall conclusion of my analysis is that this paradox can be transcended by using the insights and strategeis of such theorists as Derrida, Althusser, and Fish without remaining committed to the necessity for an overarching explanation, a systematic definition of the *nature* of the relationship between social life and discourse. Perhaps if we recognize the variety and the mutability of the forms in which this relationship is actualized, there will be no more limiting and contaminating circumstances to rescue literature from. Informed by a more dialogic view of societies, communities, and ideologies, we can discuss literature's involvement in them without the fear of compromising its value.

Such a discussion must be able to account for the real, concrete circumstances of the production and the reception of literary texts, and to reveal the mechanisms through which these texts are put into the service of divergent political interests. Many attempts along these lines are already under way in literary criticism. What is called New Historicism in the United States is perhaps the clearest example of combining the insights of deconstruction, feminism, reader-response criticism and others in the direction that I have indicated in this study.

Acknowledgments

I would like to thank Oscar Kenshur, who has been a source of intellectual inspiration throughout my graduate studies in Indiana University, for his valuable contributions to the content of this book. I would also like to thank David Bleich, Matei Calinescu, and Barbara Klinger for helpful comments and advice.

Gürol Irzık contributed to my work with unfailing encouragement and generous sacrifices. Emrah Irzık shared my interest in words and stories, and took pride in my work.

I am grateful to the Graduate School of Indiana University for supporting my research through a dissertation year fellowship.

DECONSTRUCTION AND THE POLITICS OF CRITICISM

CHAPTER 1

INTRODUCTION

> ... a (any) society may be stabilized only if it excludes poetic language. Murder, death, and unchanging society represent precisely the inability to hear and understand the signifier as such--as ciphering, as rhythm, as a presence that precedes the signification of object or emotion. The poet is put to death because he wants to turn rhythm into a dominant element; because he wants to make language perceive what it doesn't want to say, provide it with its matter independently of the sign, and free it from denotation. For it is this eminently parodic gesture that changes the system. (Julia Kristeva, *Desire in Language*, 31)

It is typical of the rhetoric of deconstructionist criticism to employ terms of power and freedom with a tone of urgency and of rebellion. "System," "ideology," "stability" are only a few examples of the elements this rhetoric represents as being engaged in the repression of "free play," "plurality," "poetry," and other forces of liberation in a struggle where even "death" and "murder" seem to have a place, if only figuratively. This apparent drama of power and freedom, of repression and transgression, combined with the equally common claim that deconstruction is a method of demystification, a way of "making language perceive what it doesn't want to say," makes it quite possible to see a political dimension in deconstructionist writing.

Jacques Derrida and other deconstructionists interpret texts in ways that reverse accepted hierarchies, promoting the marginal over the central, the fragment over the whole, in an attempt to turn the text against itself and to expose its silent assumptions. Thus, the apparent ability of these critics to subvert the logic by which particular systems of thought establish their authority, coupled with their insistence on the radical indeterminacy of linguistic signs and the unlimited plurality of the meanings of texts, creates the impression that there is a necessary relationship between their epistemological claims and ideological analyses. My purpose in this study is to ascertain whether such a logical relationship indeed exists, and to use this question as a point of departure for discussing whether the principles of deconstruction, as they are developed in the works of Jacques Derrida, provide useful categories and strategies for viewing literary texts and criticism in a political context.

I believe that this is an important question because in spite of the apparently increasing concern for the social contexts of knowledge and discourse in contemporary philosophy as well as literary theory, we have not as yet developed a fruitful way of speaking about the involvement of texts in the lives of communities. With a degree of schematization, most of the attempts that have so far been made in this direction can be seen as falling into one of two categories: either a text is relegated to a social realm called "ideology" and the critic exposes its ideological nature by analyzing it "scientifically;" or the text is alleged to be what a community of readers or interpreters makes of it, and the critic goes on with the usual business of making something of it, saving talk about communities for meta-critical discourse. In the first case more energy goes into trying to establish the scientific status of the analysis than doing the actual analysis, and in the second case the assertion of the communal character of literature does not amount to much more than a theoretical safeguard against the anarchy of pure subjectivism.

The interesting thing about the political discourse of deconstruction is that it does not fall into either one of these categories. Derrida's critique of representation and his refusal to privilege one discourse over another provide convincing arguments for avoiding the ideology/science dichotomy. The famous deconstructionist dictum that "there is nothing outside the text," whatever its own paradoxes might be, is an important challenge to models of false representations and distorted reflections. On the other hand, the notions of ideological assumptions, the socially committed nature of all branches of discourse and of the very acts of reading and writing play important and very functional roles in most deconstructionist readings of individual texts. Even in such reader-oriented examples as Barthes' later works, the idea of the social involvement of the text goes beyond agreement or disagreement within a narrowly defined community of readers. At least upon first glance, deconstruction seems to be able to avoid the two extremes of social determinism and subjectivism while incorporating the advantages of both.

If all this is indeed true, the potential of deconstructionist theory to give us an epistemologically consistent strategy for ideological analyses of texts, and a new understanding of the politics of reading, writing, and criticism is worth exploring. In order to do this, it is necessary to identify and discuss the different ways in which deconstruction might be viewed as having ultimately political implications, on both theoretical and practical levels.

Most discussions of the politics of deconstruction have been concerned with deducing its political motivations and/or consequences from its philosophical premises and its views about the indeterminacy of linguistic meaning. This strategy is used by its severest critics as well as its most enthusiastic defenders. In its simplest form, this line of thinking takes as its point of departure the idea that deconstruction, like several other modern critical schools, attacks the premise that there is one stable, objective text or reality which a knowing subject or an interpreter is obliged to represent as accurately as possible.

According to political analyses sympathetic to deconstruction, such an objective text or reality is nothing but a myth, and debunking it amounts to subverting the authorty, not only of the text or the real, but also of the individuals and the institutions that claim to have privileged access to them. If there is no truth, and thus no such privileged access to it, everyone is in principle free to act according to his or her interests and needs. Especially in the realm of literary studies, the decline of the authority of the text means freedom for the reader and greater respect for the multiplicity of interpretations, concerns, discourses. Moreover, literary institutions are not the only ones that have been built on the false and opressive ideal of objective, unchanging, univocal truths. Logocentrism, according to this view, has always been in complicity with the mechanisms of domination and exclusion throughout Western culture. To oppose it philosophically is also to oppose the oppressive, authoritarian forces it serves.

On the other hand, those who are critical of deconstruction and related post-structuralist views about knowledge and interpretation reason that forsaking the ideal of truth would result in not subverting but further legitimizing the authority of those already in power. Individuals or groups who would like to challenge established forms of authority would be deprived of the philosophical, logical arguments that would lend support to such a challenge in the name of truth, human nature, universal justice, and other "logocentric" concepts. In the realm of scientific or literary interpretation, forsaking objectivity and the ideal of correctness would remove all rational obstacles against putting knowledge into the service of dominant political and economic interests.

The sheer volume of writing that has been devoted to arguing one side or the other of this issue is a good indication that it is ultimately unresolvable. Indeed, several recent discussions of the subject have been very enlightening in their explanations of why it is so. Through a critique of Michael Ryan's ideological analysis of Hobbes' "logocentrism" in Ryan's *Marxism and Deconstruction*, for example, Oscar Kenshur concludes that "no epistemological position can be *intrinsically* reactionary or *intrinsically* progressive" (347) since "a single epistemological stance can be used to support divergent sectional interests," and "the same sectional interests can be served by surprisingly divergent epistemological claims" ("Demystifying the Demystifiers," 350). He illustrates this principle by showing how Hobbes, whose theory of "proper" language Ryan deconstructs, uses surprisingly similar "deconstructionist" ideas to attack his own political rivals, with both writers putting themselves on the side of mediation and deferral against their opponents' claims of absolute presence.

In "The Pseudo-Politics of Interpretation" Gerald Graff defends the same position and clarifies several confusions that have arisen because of the current theorizing about the politics of criticism. He groups these confusions under three categories as problems of relevance, of specificity, and of adequacy. With respect to relevance, he points out that "the fact that a literary theory may result in good or bad social consequences is logically irrelevant to its cogency as a theory" (147). Even though knowledge and its uses cannot be apolitical, objectionable political consequences do not prove a theory false, just as

> Those who protest agaist war-related research don't claim that the research is epistemologically invalidated by the political uses to which it is put, that is, they wouldn't claim that the principles of ballistics or of nuclear fission are somehow rendered less true when they are used for destructive ends. (147)

In relation to the question of specificity, Graff makes the same point as Kenshur, observing that the same theory can serve a great variety of political purposes. There is no way of deducing a specific politics from a particular theory of meaning or literature, and those who "label theories such as objectivism or deconstructionism as 'authoritarian' or 'subversive' are committing a fallacy of overspecificity" (151).

Perhaps the most neglected problem that Graff addresses in relation to discussions of the politics of literary theories is the problem of adequacy. He asks whether the political judgements that are so often made about linguistic or literary theories are based on an adequate analysis of social practices. When literary critics use such terms as interest, authority, community, or even more specific ones like liberalism or technocracy, they almost always assume that the meanings of these terms are self evident and agreed upon by all who use them. This seems ironic since attentiveness to the contexts of words and the variations in their meanings is presumably a second nature to any student of literature. However, it is not so surprising when we consider the extreme degree of specialization within academic disciplines and the inadequacy of communication between them. Even though interdisciplinary studies are becoming increasingly popular, researchers in one field often view the other field as a reservoir of ready made concepts to be borrowed and used to support their own views rather than as areas of inquiry in which every important hypothesis or concept is as much a part of a continuing debate as in the researcher's own field. Somehow, when a literary critic uses terms that originate in sociology or economics, she feels entitled to do so with much less self-consciousness than she would feel if she had been using terms like authorial intention, implied reader, thematic unity, etc. But lack of expertise outside one's own field is hardly an excuse to continue this tradition, especially when, as Graff points out, "the theories of these critics and philosophers are often strongly conditioned, if not strictly determined, by their sociological premises" (153).

The conclusion I draw from Graff's cautionary remarks is that to study the political aspects of criticism, especially with reference to deconstruction, is not to attribute political consequences to epistemological and linguistic theories, but to make the critics' own assumptions about the nature of social practices explicit and to explore the potential their approaches have for making these practices relevant to the study of literary texts, and conversely, making the study of texts relevant to an understanding of social practices. Again as Graff points out, this is "as much a matter of empirical investigation as of logical analysis" (153).

Before going on to consider what such an investigation might involve, though, I would like to point out a certain peculiarly political *form* that deconstructionist discourse has, which to me is a revealing sign of the important difficulties we will encounter in speaking of a politics of deconstruction. It is not a coincidence that the political drama we noted in the epigraph to this chapter takes place among such figures as "poetic language," "rhythm," "the signifier," and "denotation." Although this particular passage may be a more extreme example, elements of the same drama are easy to find in all types of similar assertions. For instance, talking about "differance," Derrida says that,

> It commands nothing, rules over nothing, and nowhere does it exercise any authority. It is not marked by a capital letter. Not only is there no realm of differance, but differance is even the subversion of every realm. This is obviously what makes it threatening and necessarily dreaded by everything in us that desires a realm, the past or future presence of a realm. ("Differance," 153)

The threatening, subversive "differance" that seems to be capable of commanding, ruling, exercising authority, but refuses to do so, like

Kristeva's "rhythm" or Barthes' "writerly," is an example of a peculiar sort of personification that can hardly be viewed as a mere figure of speech. While deliberately leaving human subjects outside the discussion, deconstructionist discourse attributes not only ideological values, but even powers of repression and subversion to epistemological and linguistic categories rather than specific ideas. There is, of course, an elaborate epistemology behind this attitude. It is closely related to the dissolution of the concept of individual subjects, the idea that language games operate quite independently of the players. We will have occasion to examine these notions in detail later on. But whatever the philosophical validity of these positions, the fact remains that the intensity with which deconstructionists "politicize" linguistic and literary terms does not necessarily indicate the usefulness of their approach for studying literature and language in a social context. While discussing the relationships between deconstructionist criticism and the ideological analysis of texts then, it would be best to bypass the liberationist rhetoric in which the conceptual apparatus of this type of criticism is often articulated.

When we thus refuse to concentrate on the aspects of deconstruction that have been most visible in the discussions of its politics, is there still a politics of deconstruction left to talk about, without simply invoking the cliché that everything is political? I believe that there is, and a number of approaches to the issue remain possible. First, we have to acknowledge that the lack of a necessary relationship between epistemology and ideology does not invalidate all types of logical analysis concerning the political implications of a theory. Declaring concepts like indeterminacy, differance, trace, etc. intrinsically revolutionary or reactionary is not justifiable, but one can still explore the suitability of these concepts and others like them for the type of ideological analysis one is interested in performing. Such exploration becomes especially meaningful and important as one proceeds to examine more specific deconstructionist principles such as the return of the excluded term, the structurality of all centers, or the reversibility of all hierarchies. These principles might not have political implications in themselves, but they may or may not prove to be useful methods of analysis in the context of specific political concerns.

These and other main strategies of deconstruction have indeed been discussed in political terms by writers with different political concerns. Those who would like to see it as a valuable instrument for ideological demystification point out, for example, that the type of attention to language fostered by deconstructionism unmasks acts of exclusion and subordination which are made to seem automatic and natural by the patterns of our language and the other representational schemes that we encounter and use every day. They see the philosophical deconstruction of hierarchical oppositions as an ideological tool to challenge existing social hierarchies. For example, deconstructionist feminists have in various ways demonstrated how dominant male discourses can be dismantled by identifying and overturning the binary oppositions that regulate them.

On the other hand, critics of deconstruction have often declared it politically impotent because of its separation from practice, its eradication of a purposive subject, its resignation to necessity, and impoverishment of action. An especially popular charge has been that it is just another form of New Criticism that restricts itself to the scene of discourse, denying the possibility of any realm other than that of the text, and treating the products of different historical situations as all parts of one idealized, general text. Frank Lentricchia, for example, claims that "Derrida's deconstructive project is formalist through and through" (*After the New Criticism*, 177), and that his followers often lead us to a "realm of the thoroughly predictable linguistic transcendental, where literature speaks synchronically and endlessly the same tale" (317).

At the risk of some eclecticism I agree, in part, with both of these positions. What is called deconstruction is a heterogenous mass of writing, an only loosely defined genre of philosophizing and criticism that is comprehensive enough to inhabit opposing interests, tendencies, and political characteristics. Moreover, even if deconstructionist criticism were more uniform and clear-cut, it would be possible to show both of the above characterizations to be applicable to it, since they are not necessarily incompatible. This does not mean that analyses of this type are pointless, but it does indicate that in order to be more conclusive, they should be supported by more empirical investigations, taking into account the choices that are made by deconstructionists under specific circumstances with specific purposes.

There have, of course, been several references to the actual political pronouncements and alignments of deconstructionist theorists in the discussion of the politics of deconstruction. Jacques Derrida's leftist sympathies as well as the more conservative beliefs of the Yale deconstructionists have received some attention. A more informative account along similar veins is Nancy Frazer's exposition of the political debates among French followers of Derrida in "The French Derridians: Politicizing Deconstruction or Deconstructing the Political." Positions articulated in this debate range from seeing deconstruction in the service of a "revolution more radical than has ever been conceived, one which celebrates differance as 'absolute danger' and 'the monstrosity of the future'" (133), to refusing "the very genre of political debate" (142). Frazer herself characterizes the Center for Philosophical Research on the Political, the institute in which these positions were debated, as "a temporary waystation on the exodus from Marxism now being traveled by the French intelligentsia" (154). Although these observations are indeed elements of an empirical investigation, they are to a large extent irrelevant to my concern with deconstruction as a form of textual analysis. I choose, instead, to see and evaluate deconstructionist criticism as a research program. I am not interested in evaluating the political expediency of deconstruction in general, but in questioning the ability of deconstructionist criticism to perform a rather specific task: to provide a methodology for analyzing texts as social phenomena, from the viewpoint of their involvement in social conflicts. I am aware that most deconstructionists would object to the term methodology, but this is an issue that can be taken up later.

Although such questions as the textualism of deconstruction or its conception of the individual subject are still highly relevant to the type of evaluation I am proposing, it would not be very useful to consider these questions in isolation and to try to decide their merits independently of what has already been done in the area of political criticism. I believe that one effective strategy to combine theoretical and empirical considerations in exploring the potential of deconstruction for a political criticism is to start by viewing it in its relation to other theoretical frameworks within which the social aspects of texts have been formulated. After all, a research program can be evaluated only in the context of preceding and alternative programs, considering whether it explains more, yields better practical results, offers novel solutions to existing problems, etc. This is why I am going to start by exploring the relationships between Derrida's theoretical premises and the concept of ideology, the single theoretical category under whose aegis perhaps the majority of all political analyses of texts have been attempted. Later, I will use the deconstructionists' critique of the "humanist" assumptions about individual subjects to bring this theory into contact with more practical concerns such as those of feminist criticism. Finally, I will consider the usefulness of another important concept that seems to have a potential to tie literary texts to the social environment in which they are interpreted, if not produced: the concept of an interpretive community.

CHAPTER 2

DECONSTRUCTING IDEOLOGY

What is perhaps in the process of being reconsidered is the form of closure that was called "ideology" (doubtless a concept to be analyzed in its function, its history, its origins, its transformations), the form of the relationships between a transformed concept of "infrastructure," if you will--an "infrastructure" of which the *general text* would no longer be an effect or a reflection--and the transformed concept of "ideology." . . . What is produced in the current trembling is a reevaluation of the relationship between the general text and what was believed to be, in the form of reality (history, politics, economics, sexuality, etc.), the simple, referable exterior of language or writing, the belief that this exterior could operate from the simple position of cause or accident. (Derrida, *Positions*, 90-91)

    Ideology is a term very frequently encountered in all forms of political criticism, be it Marxist, feminist, or conservative. It is also encountered almost as frequently in the types of criticism that purport to be uncontaminated by the political, the dismissal of ideology being equivalent to the assertion of the "purity" of both literary and critical discourses. In fact, "ideological" is often used interchangeably with "political," especially in relation to the analysis and criticism of cultural phenomena. In stark contrast to the almost universal assumption that the term "political" is self-explanatory, however, there has been little agreement upon what an ideology is or what constitutes ideological criticism.
    The main reason for this should be sought not so much in some intrinsic difficulty in the concept as in the fact that it has traditionally served as the focus of epistemological debates concerning the status of

political discourse. Definitions of ideology are not simply methodological introductions providing conceptual tools for analysis. They are also, and perhaps primarily, a series of claims about the validity of one's own discourse in relation to that of the discourse being analyzed. The traditionally accepted opposition between science and ideology, and the Marxist definition of ideology as "false consciousness" are only the most obvious examples of this type of claim in which one discourse theorizes its categorical difference from the other and thus tries to demonstrate its invulnerability to its own critique. Ideological talk, like all talk about language, is inescapably self-referential, but it is also a struggle for escaping or transcending that self-referentiality.

If the notion of ideology is indeed the locus of a power struggle between different discourses, and deconstruction is a radical reevaluation of the terms in which such struggles are fought out, a deconstructive critique and transformation of the notion of ideology, such as the one Derrida outlines in the epigraph to this chapter, would have important consequences, not only for the theory and practice of ideological analysis, but also for the enterprise of deconstruction itself. In order to determine the political dimensions of deconstructionist writing then, it will be useful to bring it in contact with a theory of ideology, to return once more to the epistemological and the practical problems surrounding the concept of ideology, and to see if the deconstructive strategies of Derrida's philosophy would lead to fruitful transformations of this concept or undermine it altogether.

Although Derrida rarely mentions the term "ideology," and he does not derive political consequences from philosophical stances as readily as some of his followers, several central notions in his writing correspond to the most fundamental concerns of theories of ideology. Perhaps the most obvious of these are his views about representation, the status of the subject, and, I believe, the notion of deconstruction itself, with its connotations of exposing and subverting. Althusser's theory of ideology is especially suitable for a comparison with Derrida's philosophy because it is centered on precisely these notions. But to see the function and significance of these notions in Althusser's theory it is necessary to have an understanding of earlier Marxist discussions of ideology, how he develops them and departs from them.

The Classical Marxist Conception of Ideology

According to the classical Marxist view, exemplified most clearly in Marx's *German Ideology*, ideology is a relationship between the object and the subject structured in such a way that the subject is unable to recognize the true relationship between material reality and consciousness:

> If in all ideology men and their circumstances appear upside down as in a *camera obscura*, this phenomenon arises just as much from their historical life process as the inversion of objects on the retina does from their physical life process. (*German Ideology*, 14)

Ideology, then, is a vision of the world that is standing upside down. The meaning of this is that in all ideology, ideas and beliefs are seen as the sources of material processes instead of being recognized as the reflections of these processes. A similar idea is more elaborately expressed by Engels:

> Ideology is a process accomplished by the so-called thinker, consciously indeed, but with a false consciousness. The real motives impelling him remain unknown to him, otherwise it would not be an ideological process at all. Hence he imagines false or apparent motives. Because it is a process of thought he derives both its form and its content from pure thought, either his own or that of his predecessors. (*Marx and Engels on Art and Literature*, 99)

Used in this rather general sense, ideology is almost synonymous with philosophical idealism as seen by materialists. In his discussion of "Althusser and the Theory of Ideology" Paul Hirst points out that this conception of ideology as false consciousness is based on an empiricist subject/object structure in which "experience either corresponds to the nature of the object or misrecognizes it" (386). Marx and Engels concentrate on a sort of "built-in" lack of ability in the thinker to determine his or her true relationship with the real, and thus to have a correct perception of it. The disability is built-in because it is a product of the thinker's position in society, the angle from which he or she perceives reality. Thus the phenomenon of ideology arises from the subject's "historical life process" in the same spontaneous way, and with the same determinism, as "the inversion of objects on the retina does from their physical life process."

However, Marx and Engels do not always discuss ideology in terms of a spontaneous process of the production of ideas. They also clearly define it as a conscious and purposeful activity of producing false beliefs to serve the interests of the ruling classes. Thus,

> The division of labour, which we saw above as one of the chief forces of history up till now, manifests itself also in the ruling class as the division of mental and material labor, so that inside this class one

> part appears as the thinkers of the class (its active, conceptive ideologists, who make the perfecting of the illusion of the class about itself their chief source of livelihood), while the others' attitude to these ideas and illusions is more passive and receptive, because in reality they are the active members of this class and have less time to make up illusions and ideas about themselves. (39-40)

There are active ideologists, then, whose specific function in society is to produce illusions about the ruling classes and society in general.

This view may not be totally at odds with the definitions we considered above. It retains the notion of ideology as a distorted reflection of the real in its emphasis on the idea of illusions. Although there is a clear difference in tone and emphasis between the deterministic, spontaneous nature of the ideological process in the earlier description and the systematic, deliberate activity outlined here, it would be too mechanical to see this as an absolute contradiction. Active ideologists may be seen as being engaged in developing and articulating a representation of the world whose necessarily distorted character is a given. They may be more or less conscious of their social motives in preferring certain representations to others, and the ways in which they articulate those representations are not fully dictated by their class positions. This does not mean that they could in fact choose to transcend the "historical life process" which makes it necessary that "in all ideology men and their circumstances appear upside down." The "falseness" of ideology is structurally determined, but its production and transformations are not automatic. Thus it is possible to say that the "camera obscura" view of ideology is not totally irreconcilable with the notion of a consciously and systematically developed class ideology. Nevertheless, it is important to keep in mind that there is a tension here because the question of just how active and how much in control individuals are in constructing, articulating, and changing their ideological positions is of central importance for evaluating Derrida's philosophy of language and perception as well as Althusser's theory of ideology.

There is also a related tension between the predominantly epistemological definition of ideology as philosophical idealism and the more functional and political terms in which it is put forth as being characteristic of a certain class or as denoting an entire system of legal, political, religious, and aesthetic forms determined by an economic foundation. For example, when Marxist theoreticians such as Lenin refer to a "working class ideology," sometimes they mean the sum total of ideas and attitudes that this class acquires as a result of being active in production, and sometimes they mean socialist theory itself, formulated by the intelligentsia and introduced to the working class from without. In any case, they do not mean false consciousness, the inverted world view of the bourgeois thinker to whom "the real motives impelling him remain unknown." Similarly, when the phrase "ideological formations" is used to distinguish legal, political, religious and other cultural institutions from economic structures that are said to determine them, it seems to refer to the entire process of idea-formation in a society, regardless of content, correspondence to reality, or class character.

It is possible to provide arguments that would give the classical Marxist discussions of ideology more consistency than they seem to have according to my account. One could mention the Marxist principle that the ruling ideas in any society are the ideas of the ruling class, and assert that the contradictions I pointed out above are significantly reduced by this unifying claim. Such an argument would maintain that as long as we are talking about a class society, the superstructure as a whole will serve to legitimate the power of the ruling class in society, and thus bring together the class character, the "falseness," and the more generally superstructural sense of ideology.

Nevertheless, I do not believe that the fundamental tensions between the different usages of ideology within Marxist discourse can be fully removed by any ingenuity of argument. Even if it were possible to find a neat theoretical reconciliation among these usages, difficulties would be apparent at the level of more specific analyses. Indeed, even a casual examination of Marxist proclamations about "ideological formations" like art and science reveals a number of difficulties. For example, how can science be ideological and still provide an accurate understanding of the world, if ideology is indeed false consciousness? On the other hand, how can it not be ideological if it is part of a superstructure in which there are no neutral elements, and if it is an established, powerful social institution in a social structure in which the ruling ideas are the ideas of the ruling class? Also, considering all this, what does it mean to say that Marxism itself is scientific, or that it can provide a scientific critique of ideologies? These questions and several parallel ones concerning art and other cultural phenomena have been asked by Marxists as well as critics of Marxism, and there have been very fruitful attempts to go beyond simplistic oppositions between science and ideology. The Frankfurt School treatment of science, especially in the works of Theodor Adorno and Max Horkheimer, is a good example of such an attempt. In *The Dialectics of Enlightenment* Adorno and Horkheimer analyze the notion of scientific rationality itself as an instance of ideology, reflecting a concern of the Frankfurt School in general. However, most Marxist theories of ideology still oscillate between the negative and the positive, the economical and the political, the active and the passive definitions of the term.

I would argue that the main source of these difficulties is the desire to make the concept of ideology serve double, or rather triple duty on epistemological, political and sociological levels of analysis. It would be absurd to deny that there are interrelationships between these levels, but they are complex relationships, and clearly not those of logical entailment or linear, one sided determinations. Although at a certain level of generality an ideological position can be shown to represent the interests of a particular class, the specific content of an ideology can never be directly determined by that class or by the membership of the individual ideologist in that class. Moreover, specific political analyses, such as the highly original and persuasive ones performed by Marx himself in *The Eighteenth Brumaire of Louis Bonaparte* clearly show that there is no homogeneity between classes in the strict economical or "infrastructural" sense and specific ideologies. The same class interests can be served by very different ideologies in different historical situations, or sections of an economical class can adopt opposing ideological positions in the context of a narrow political struggle. Other struggles such as those against racism or for women's liberation cut across economic class distinctions, and the ideological forms in which these struggles are fought out clearly cannot be reduced to pre-existing class positions from which reality is viewed.

As a matter of fact, several contemporary political movements, and most notably feminism, strongly indicate that there are no relationships of anteriority or posteriority between political forces and the ideologies that serve them. Although women have always existed, they are only recently emerging as a political force by actively constructing new voices, worldviews, oppositional strategies and the like, reconstituting themselves and redefining their social existence in the process. In *On Deconstruction* Jonathan Culler observes that "to ask a woman to read as a woman is in fact a double or divided request. It appeals to the condition of being a woman as if it were a given and simultaneously urges that this condition be created or achieved" (49). This is not as much of a paradox as it seems. It is only one example of how the very existence of a group of people as an agent in the history of a society depends on ideological and political conditions rather than political life being determined by already-formed classes or naturally given groups. In *The Crisis in Historical Materialism* Stanley Aronowitz suggests that classes exist not as inevitable configurations constituted by an "infrastructure," but only insofar as they are formed within the context of an economic, ideological and political struggle (73-110).

These considerations show that it is not possible to treat the term ideology as a focal point around which homologies among epistemological, political, and sociological analyses can be built in the framework of a materialist metaphysics. There is no continuity between the pairs: objective position/subjective perception; economic class/ideology; infrastructure/superstructure; where the first determines the second, at least "in the last analysis." It does not even take such considerations to see that defining ideology as false and science as true does not facilitate ideological analysis, especially if we keep in mind the controversies in the philosophy of science about the nature and possibility of scientific truth. However, before discussing this particular issue any further, we should consider whether Althusser's conception of ideology avoids the difficulties we encountered in the classical Marxist uses of the term. For, as Derrida says, it would be useful to analyze the notion of ideology in its transformations before transforming it once more.

Althusser and the Theory of Ideology

In "Ideology and Ideological State Apparatuses" Althusser defines ideology primarily by its function. Since every social formation has to reproduce its own conditions of production, its survival depends on the constant reproduction of both the productive forces and the existing relations of production. An important part of this process is the reproduction of labor power,

> which requires not only a reproduction of its skills, but also, at the same time, a reproduction of its submission to the rules of the established order, i. e. a reproduction of submission to the ruling ideology for the workers, and a reproduction of the ability to manipulate the ruling ideology correctly for the agents of exploitation and repression, so that they, too, will provide for the domination of the ruling class "in words." (132-33)

In other words, the exploited have to learn to submit while the agents of exploitation have to learn how to use and retain their power.

From this initial account ideology emerges as being much more actively and purposefully produced than the 'camera obscura' image would seem to suggest. Paul Hirst points out that this is a departure from the classical Marxist treatment of ideology as a distorted reflection of the real in consciousness ("Althusser and the Theory of Ideology," 186-88). In Althusser's account, unlike that in *The German Ideology*, ideology is not directly derived from the position of the subject in relation to the real. Althusser sees ideology as a means of *constituting* the subjects in such a way as to insure that the existing economic and social relations will continue to exist. Referring to Althusser's famous definition of ideology as "a representation of the imaginary relationship of individuals to their real conditions of existence" ("ISA," 162), Hirst goes on to explain that

Althusser's definition of individual subjects rejects the empiricist model in which an already constituted individual consciousness experiences a reality that remains outside it and "present" to it. Instead, people relate to the real conditions of their existence in an imaginary mode through which they themselves are formed as subjects. This imaginary mode is not a set of illusions, it is a social condition, a "definite structure of recognition" in which conditions of existence are posited and lived "as if" they were given. Ideology is the representation of this imaginary mode.

By redefining the notions of object and subject then, Althusser seems to have dispensed with the empiricist dimension of the theory of ideology that we observed in the case of classical Marxism. When the object, i.e. the real, is defined as what can only be experienced in an "imaginary" mode by a subject that is constituted by that experience, the problem of the correspondence or lack of correspondence between the object and the subject does indeed disappear. If ideology is not a form of consciousness, much less a false one, an ideological critique need not be burdened by the task of refuting ideology through a comparison to the real and then trying to show that the critic has better access to the real. In order to analyze a representational system ideologically, it should be sufficient to show how it provides individuals with a total picture of their own relations to their "conditions of existence," how it presents these relations as given, and how it thus assigns the individuals to their places within those conditions of existence.

But what does this mean? According to Althusser "there is no practice except by and in an ideology;" and "there is no ideology except by the subject and for subjects" (165). Ideology is what makes social practices possible by involving individuals in them as subjects in both senses of the word. For example, a racist ideology is not only a series of assertions about the inferiority of a particular race, but also a series of practices such as segregation which assign different roles to different people, and symbolic structures that reinforce both the assertions and the practice. People are constituted as subjects in these practices insofar as there is no "black" or "white" person in any significant sense outside or before an ideology that is built upon the exclusion and the repression of the black race. Thus,

> Like all obviousnesses, including those that make a word 'name a thing' or 'have a meaning' (therefore including the obviousness of the 'transparency of language'), the obviousness that you and I are subjects--and that that does not cause any problems--is an ideological effect, the elementary ideological effect. (171-72)

Althusser's insistence on the *materiality* of ideology as social practice, and on the *function* of ideology as the perpetuation of existing social relations leads him to conceive of a whole network of institutions such as legal, educational, and religious ones, which he calls "ideological state apparatuses." While other state apparatuses such as the army and the police function primarily by "violence," that is by direct repression, ideological state apparatuses function primarily by ideology and they are distinguished from the former by their involvement in the private domains of life--such as the family--as well as the public, and their plurality as opposed to the centralized character of the others. However, this plurality does not preclude a deeper unity:

> If the ideological state apparatuses "function" massively and predominantly by ideology, what unifies their diversity is precisely this functioning, insofar as the ideology by which they function is always in fact unified, despite its diversity and its contradictions, beneath the ruling ideology, which is the ideology of the ruling class. (146)

Through his redefinition of the subject and his model of the ideological state apparatuses, Althusser implicitly abandons the reflectionist theory of ideology and the infrastructure/superstructure distinction on which it is based. Even though he retains the terms of the distinction and explains the necessity for ideology primarily through its economic function, ideology for him is not a distorted reflection of the real, but a means of its perpetuation. It is not a false consciousness that can be opposed to a true one. And although he does allow for the possibility of being situated outside ideology, this possibility is not one of having direct access to the real, of simply recognizing it instead of misrecognizing it.

On the other hand, the tendency of classical Marxism to use the notion of ideology to create homologies between different levels of analysis such as the epistemological, political and sociological is hardly absent in Althusser. I noted earlier that he avoided defining ideology as an epistemological phenomenon by refusing to see the knowing subject as existing independently of the object of its knowledge. In this way, he was able to do without the untenable requirement that ideology be a function of the noncorrespondence between the object and the subject, that it be "false." Nevertheless, his notion of ideology is negative and absolute enough that he still needs to posit a science that is simply defined by its opposition to ideology. If it is not the direct experience of the real, the true consciousness that can be opposed to the false one, it is the subject-less discourse that can be opposed to the one that is only "by and for a subject," i.e. ideology. Thus he can say that

> the author, insofar as he writes the lines of a discourse which claims to be scientific, is completely absent as a 'subject' from 'his' scientific discourse (for all scientific discourse is by definition a subject-less discourse, there is no 'Subject of science' except in an ideology of science). (171)

The obvious question is how such a discourse is possible when the only alternative to being a subject, by Althusser's explicit account, is being a presocial, "abstract" individual, and when even the unborn child is already a subject in the sense that it will be born into an ideology that has already assigned it a family name, a certain sexual identity, etc. Right before the passage just quoted, Althusser makes a point of stating that he as a writer and we as readers are still and inevitably in ideology as we try to attain knowledge of it. The only apparent way in which these statements can be reconciled is to draw the conclusion that the creation of a scientific discourse is tantamount to a self-consciousness that "erases" one's "subjecthood" from that discourse, even if the discourse could not be possible without that subjecthood. That is, even though it is not possible to *live* outside ideology, to *live* as anything but a subject, it is possible, in certain contexts, to pull oneself up by the epistemological bootstraps and to *know* ideology, from without, in science.

But it is a naive optimism to think that self-consciousness can lead to true knowledge. Being aware of the fact that one has an ideology, that one can never be completely free of prejudices, unscientific beliefs, unconscious motives, and the like is an important, but a general, abstract awareness. It is not a guarantee against the possibility that these prejudices, beliefs, motives may in fact be determining one's perception in specific cases, or even one's ideological self-consciousness itself. It is not even a guarantee that they can be identified in each case by the subject who harbors them. No amount of theoretical knowledge of ideology or prejudice can assure a scientist, for example, that his findings in the laboratory have not been influenced by his political beliefs, economic interests, racial background, etc. Karl Popper goes as far as to say that "not only does self-analysis not help us to overcome the unconscious determination of our views, it often leads to even more subtle self-deception." In the same context, he observes that "those who are most convinced of having got rid of their prejudices are most prejudiced" (*The Open Society*, 223). This is not cause to despair, but it is cause to construct scientific practice in such a way that there will be checks and balances against such influences. In any event, when Althusser says that "It is necessary to be outside ideology, i.e. in scientific knowledge, to be able to say: I am in ideology (a quite exceptional case) or (the general case): I was in ideology" (175), the "exceptional case" is as paradoxical as it sounds, and the "general case" begs the question because his theory asserts the impossibility of leaving ideology behind.

Even if we disregard the science/ideology dichotomy that creates these paradoxes, the absoluteness of Althusser's characterization of ideological state apparatuses and human subjects leaves hardly any room for a possibility of a critique of ideologies. If his scientism continues the Marxist tradition of unifying ideologies under the umbrella of everything that is not science, his model of ideological state apparatuses continues the tendency to see "superstructure" as a homogeneous totality. Even though these apparatuses are characterized by plurality and lack of strict centralization, even though they override the distinctions between the public and the private, the material and the mental, they are nevertheless unified "insofar as the ideology by which they function is always in fact unified, despite its diversity and its contradictions, *beneath the ruling ideology*" (146). We noted earlier that the same appeal to the ruling ideology becomes necessary whenever one's desire to see a unity between economy, politics, social institutions, and knowledge is so strong that it cannot accommodate an account of the lack of correspondence between these levels or an account of competing ideologies.

But if we tried to show that seemingly diverse ideological structures and apparatuses are indeed unified beneath the ruling ideology in Althusser's terms, we would be led into a tautology. Althusser does not offer a definition of ruling ideology other than that it is the ideology of the ruling class. Since, according to his definition, ideology is what ensures the reproduction of existing relations of production, it could not serve the interests of any group other than the ruling classes, the classes that profit from the existing relations of production. Ideology cannot be anything but a ruling ideology. Thus, Althusser's definition of ideology already assumes the unity that he later claims for ideological state apparatuses and seems to justify by his appeal to the unity of the ruling ideology.

The same desire for unity and closure is evident in the characterization of the subject. Ideology is so totally repressive and unified, and the formation of the subject through repression in ideology is so complete that individuals and social groups are practically deprived of any means to resist dominant ideologies and construct alternatives. Individuals become subjects only by being "interpellated" by ideology. That is, what gives them their identity, what makes it possible for them to experience the real, is the same ideology that insures the preservation of existing social relations. Althusser's excessive theoritization of ideology thus takes to an extreme a tendency already present in Marxism; namely, the tendency to dehistoricize ideology by giving it a structural definition in terms of a subject/object dichotomy. John Higgins is right in claiming that,

> In fact, Althusser's "concrete subject," the subject of ideology and interpellation, is a very strong form of the unified subject, the only difference from the position of Cartesian certitude being that the terms of the subject's unity in Althusser's theory are terms of misrecognition. ("Raymond Williams and the Problem of Ideology," 116)

As a consequence of this unity of the subject and the unity between ideology and the subject,

> at the same time as identifying the ideological as a discrete instance for political struggle, [Althusser] also defined the ideological in such a way as to make the idea of effective struggle in the ideological domain impossible. For Althusser, language is always subjection, and never a matter of agency. (118)

Clearly, such a "monological" theory of ideology and individuals' encounters with it defeats its own purposes. It might be claimed, however, in accordance with the principle that political consequences of a theory are irrelevant to its validity, that even if such a theory is not politically expedient, it might nevertheless be true. In rejecting Althusser's account of individuals' complete subjection to repressive ideologies because of its undesirable consequences, we may be committing a logical fallacy. But although it is true that Althusser's theory defies its own political logic, my objection to his conception of ideology and human subjects is not merely ideological or pragmatic. I am not saying that his definition of ideology makes resistance and freedom impossible. I am saying that it is not capable of accounting for the amount of resistance and freedom that exists. The value of the term ideology as an analytical tool is severely limited if it explains subjection but not dissent, unity but not struggle.

The paradoxes of Althusser's theory with respect to this question are so exemplary that they provide an especially good context for a discussion of parallel difficulties in the ideological analysis of literary texts, as well as an evaluation of what deconstruction has to contribute to this enterprise.

Ideology and the Deconstruction of Metaphysics

When Althusser says that "from within ideology we have to outline a discourse which tries to break with ideology, in order to dare to be the beginning of a scientific (i.e.subjectless) discourse" ("ISA," 173), his statement, perhaps with the exception of the scientific tone, is very similar to Derrida's numerous pronouncements about the impossibility of being outside metaphysics, the necessity of eroding it from within. In fact, there are several points at which Althusser's language is strikingly Derridian. He speaks of individuals as "always already subjects," the "transparency of language" as an ideological effect, the impossibility of reality being "present" to consciousness or of the subject being "present" to itself, and the lack of a center in individual consciousness or in discourse. In an article about Lacan which was written a few years before the essay on "Ideology and Ideological State Apparatuses," he says that

> Freud has discovered for us that the real subject, the individual in his unique essence, has not the form of an ego, centred on the "ego," on "consciousness" or on "existence"--whether this is the existence of the for-itself, of the body-proper or of "behavior"--, that the human subject is de-centred, constituted by a structure which has no "centre" either, except in the imaginary misrecognition of the "ego", i.e. in the ideological formations in which it 'recognizes' itself. ("Freud and Lacan," 218-19)

That consciousness cannot serve as a stable, privileged criterion by the aid of which such "textualized" phenomena as linguistic meaning, perception, and representation can be reappropriated to a final truth, and that the very act of so privileging consciousness amounts to a socially felicitous illusion is the core of Derrida's critique of logocentrism. It is thus no coincidence that Althusser's conceptions of ideology and individual subjects have seemed particularly suitabe to post-structuralist treatments of language and culture. Althusser's former student Michel Foucault, for example, has used the idea of decentered individuals constituted by "anonymous," autonomous discourses to define power as a function of what can be said. Foucault's analyses of institutional discourses that define and thus create such phenomena as madness or criminality owe much to Althusser's conception of ideological state apparatuses.

Jacques Derrida, on the other hand, does not have a theory of ideology, and he rarely expresses any concern with specifically ideological issues. However, his writings continue to exert a remarkable influence on many contemporary critiques of culture, most notably, psychoanalysis and feminism. There have been several theoretical attempts to reconcile Derrida's philosophy with more explicitly political discourses such as Marxism. Michael Ryan's and Gayatri Spivak's writings are interesting examples of such attempts in American criticism. On the other hand, the same philosophy has generated or supported a genre of writing that is, at least upon first glance, far too playful, abstract, and self-celebratory to be useful for an understanding of such "worldly" matters as politics. Perhaps this is not totally accidental. By inserting the notion of ideology into Derrida's discourse, we might be able to locate certain tensions of the type we encountered in Althusser's case and get a better view of the sources for these divergent tendencies.

According to Derrida, the entire tradition of Western philosophy constitutes a "metaphysics of presence" which seeks to arrive at the truth of meaning, thought, reason, or being, as a foundation existing in itself. Metaphysical thinking thus rests on a structure of binary oppositions which contrast a fundamental term designating a constant or a presence with another term construed as its derivation, complication, or corruption. On the one hand, there are absolute ideals such as

> presence of the object to sight as *eidos*, presence as substance/ essence/ existence (*ousia*), temporal presence as the point (*stigme*) of the now or the instant (*nun*), self-presence of the cogito, consciousness, subjectivity, co-presence of the self and the other, intersubjectivity as an intentional phenomenon of the ego, etc. .
> (Derrida, *Of Grammatology*, 12)

On the other hand, there are their opposites conceived as secondary to those centering or grounding principles: absence, difference, deferral, language, culture, form, etc. . All metaphysicians, from Plato to Rousseau, from Descartes to Husserl, have sought to establish an origin in one of the valorized "presences" of philosophy and then to explain other phenomena as its derivations or accidents.

Deconstruction is a critique and an overturning of this metaphysics of presence. Derrida claims that there is no simple, pure, essential origin that could serve as a stable center in any system such as philosophy, language, science, or culture. As Jonathan Culler explains,

> when arguments cite particular instances of presence as grounds for further development, these instances invariably prove to be already complex constructions. What is proposed as a given, an elementary constituent, proves to be a product, dependent or derived in ways that deprive it of the authority of simple or pure presence. (*On Deconstruction*, 95)

Using this principle, Derrida and other deconstructionists locate the proposed center in every system or discourse and then undermine its centrality by showing it to be dependent on something else, to be merely one term in a continuous chain rather than an origin.

We have already been using several of Derrida's notions in criticizing the concept of ideology. For example, Derrida describes the thought proposed by his grammatology, the "science" of writing, as "the thought for which there is no sure opposition between outside and inside" (*Positions*, 12). His critique of metaphysics amounts to showing that there is no outside to language, text, and representation, from which such an entity as consciousness, empirical reality, or infrastructure could regulate them, without itself being caught up in the interplay between these elements. The oppositions between infrastructure and superstructure, production and ideology, class and ideology, material and ideological practices all fall into this definition of a metaphysical opposition between inside and outside. For example, Althusser says that "ideology *has no outside* (for itself), but at the same time it is nothing but outside (for science and reality)" ("ISA," 175). The foregoing analysis has already indicated that there is no way of maintaining these oppositions without falling into epistemological traps and putting the status of one's own discourse in question. To the extent to which ideology is defined by its being outside science and reality, Derrida's deconstruction of metaphysics undermines it as a concept. Gayatri Spivak warns, for example, that "Derrida is suspicious of the concept of ideology because, in his view, it honors too obstinate a binary opposition between mind and matter" ("The Politics of Interpretations," 260).

Indeed, the deconstruction of such an opposition and a related questioning of the very concept of representation as the name of the relationship between mind and matter has been one of the persistent themes in Derrida's writings. The term representation, in its very etymology, reveals its connection to a metaphysics of presence. Derrida explains that the classical determination of representation

> presupposes that the sign (which defers presence) is conceivable only *on the basis of* the presence that it defers and *in view of* the deferred presence one intends to reappropriate. Following this classical semiology, the substitution of the sign for the thing itself is both *secondary* and *provisional*: it is second in order after an original and lost presence, a presence from which the sign would be derived. It is provisional with respect to this final and missing presence, in view of which the sign would serve as a movement of mediation. ("Differance," 138)

He criticizes this notion of representation as a substitute for an independently existing presence by first concentrating on the notion of a sign. According to what Derrida calls the "classical semiology," the structure of a sign repeats the structure of representation. Just as a sign is a substitute for a referent, the material part of the sign, the signifier, is a substitute for its ideal content, the signified. But when we try to name and to know the signified in itself, we find that this is impossible. The signified for one signifier is only another signifier. The ideal concept is impossible independently of the chain of material signifiers. Thus,

> The first consequence to be drawn from this is that the signified concept is never present in itself, in an adequate presence that would refer only to itself. Every concept is necessarily and essentially inscribed in a chain or a system, within which it refers to another and to other concepts, by the systematic play of differences. Such a play, then--differance--is no longer simply a concept, but the possibility of conceptuality, of the conceptual system and process in general. ("Differance," 140)

"Differance" is a term Derrida uses to convey both senses of the French verb "differer": difference and deferral. "Differance" as the systematic play of differences and temporalization makes all conceptualization and thus all representation possible because signs have meaning only by virtue of differences and their signifieds are continually deferred. Just as there is no signified independently of a signifier, there is no "transcendental signified" unaffected by differance, pure and complete in itself, that could be the "presence" beyond representation. In the course of his critique of Rousseau's conception of representation as alienation, Derrida claims that metaphysics as a whole

> supposes at once that representation follows a first presence and restores a final presence. One does not ask how much of presence and how much of representation are found within presence. In criticizing representation as the loss of presence, in expecting a reappropriation of presence from it, in making it an accident or a means, one situates oneself within the self-evidence of the distinction between presentation and representation, within the *effect* of this fission. (*Of Grammatology*, 296)

Derrida is not alone in his critique of representation. The most important modern contributions to the study of culture have been made outside and against reflectionist models which assumed that representations could be understood as effects of one totality or another that preceded and contained them. Deconstructionists, as well as other contemporary theorists of culture, recognize that such cultural entities as language, knowledge, or aesthetics are not merely forms of consciousness that express, reflect, or stand for real, social, human relationships. Instead, they see them as themselves real relationships. They point out, for example, that in various ways and degrees language is constitutive of the reality that it was presumed to be representing. Such a perspective greatly facilitates the analysis of texts as they are situated "in the world," to use Edward Said's term. It relieves the analyst from grappling with the apparent paradox that any description of the "outside" of representation will have to be another representation, since it does not require comparison with such an outside for the purposes of explanation and criticism. Texts become social entities not by virtue of representing a social reality but by virtue of the uses to which they are put. They participate in power relationships by making specific categories available to public discourse and excluding others.

It is in this context that the critique of representation has been a major element in both modernist and postmodernist approaches to art and literature. It has also figured prominently in discussions of their ideological functions. For example, Jonathan Arac points out in his introduction to the collection entitled *Postmodernism and Politics*, that part of the modernist hostility to the idea of representation came about in reaction to Marxist theories of literature such as Lukacs', where a "true" representation of "real" social relationships was demanded from writers. Because most Marxist critics, like metaphysicians, believed that social reality existed in a definite and pure form outside its representations in literature, they assumed that the duty of literature was to contribute to our knowledge of this reality by representing it as faithfully as possible through artistic realism.

Although it is quite clear that Althusser does not conceive of reality as directly apprehensible, it might still seem natural to conclude that the concept of representation implicates Althusser's theory of ideology in the metaphysics that Derrida deconstructs, since Althusser defines ideology as representation. Paul Hirst's critique of Althusser provides good reasons to arrive at such a conclusion. Hirst points out, for example, that Althusser derives the unity of a social class from its economic position and then uses this model to explain the essential unity of the ideological representations of that class, even if this unity is hidden beneath a great variety of manifestations. According to Hirst, "this entails the position that classes, as social forces, exist independently of their representations by the political and ideological instances" (394). It is true that the term ideology, in Althusser's usage as well as others, has been deeply implicated in the problems arising from representational models in which there is often too great a separation between the represented and its representation. However, to underline the word representation in Althusser's definition and to conclude that this "discovery" is all that is needed to undermine his theory from a Derridian perspective would be an oversimplification of the problem. For a number of reasons, it would be an oversimplification of both Althusser's theory and Derrida's.

First, it is wrong to assume that either a theoretical critique of representation or the rejection of realism in artistic practice can situate one's discourse outside the representational paradigm. As Derrida remarks,

> to determine language [or ideology] as representation is not the effect of an accidental prejudice, a theoretical fault or a manner of thinking, a limit or closure among others, a form of representation, precisely, which came about one day and of which we could rid ourselves by a decision when the time comes. ("Sending: On Representation," 304)

Realism would best be seen as a changing set of conventions for artistic representation, not as the necessary consequence of seeing art or the entire realm of thought as representation. Since realism is not identical to or the only manifestation of the representational view of language and thought, violating realistic conventions does not amount to breaking out of representational structures. Similarly, even to characterize representation as wrong or confining, one has to represent representation, to say what it is. Simply announcing that representation is bad and then criticizing Althusser for the reliance of his theory on the concept of representation would hardly carry any weight, deconstructive or otherwise, when one did not oneself possess categories of thought not in some way or another dependent on the same concept.

Second, Derrida does not agree with the simplistic notion that "representation is bad." He warns, in "Sending: On Representation," that "the worst regressions can put themselves at the service of this anti-representative prejudice," leading to "some rehabilitation of immediacy, of original simplicity, of presence without repetition or delegation . . ." (311). In fact, as Jonathan Arac also points out, much of Derrida's deconstructive strategy has consisted of showing how everything is a representation, how there is no possibility of arriving at the (nonexistent) presence for which the representation is presumed to be a substitute. Derrida's objection to representation begins only at the point at which it becomes the name of the assumption of such a presence. He would not object to seeing ideology as representation as long as that did not imply its being determined and regulated by what it represented.

What it represents, in Althusser's case, are imaginary relations. This is the third reason why we cannot consider his theory of ideology a simple representational relation between mind and reality that would be deconstructed by Derrida's objections to such models. Althusser's imaginary is neither real nor an illusion. It is the mode in which individuals relate to their real conditions of existence. The imaginary relations represented by ideology are not opposed to "real relations" that would be represented by science. Such an opposition is not possible because the imaginary is the mode, the only possible mode, in which individuals can have any experience of the real. They cannot confront the real directly, outside the imaginary relations that make them social beings. But if this is true, the imaginary is, by Althusser's own definition, a symbolic mode, already a system of representations. It is language, image, ritual, cognition, and, necessarily, also ideology. In fact, if we follow Althusser's logic, we cannot avoid the conclusion that ideology is part of the imaginary, or better yet, an aspect of the imaginary, and not a representation of it. Ideology belongs in the imaginary because it is not only a political belief system; it is the condition of all conscious life. Althusser makes use of Lacan's imaginary to reject the "givenness" of the real and the "givenness" of the subject that experiences it. He uses the concept of ideology to show that the mediation of the imaginary is not secondary or neutral. It is constitutive and socially determined.

Thus, Althusser's definition of ideology is misleading in its seeming separation between ideology as a representation and the imaginary as what it represents. This ambiguity can be criticized. But when one recognizes that Althusser's treatment of ideology does not really obey a reflectionist model, the modernist or the deconstructionist case against representation ceases to offer a pertinent critique of that treatment. Althusser's earlier definitions of ideology as a "lived relation," and his emphasis on the constitutive effects of practices and institutions further support the point that his model is not just a complicated version of the reflectionist one. Even though Hirst is right in his diagnosis of a certain reductionism in Althusser concerning political and ideological "levels," and their relation to the economical, it would be wrong to ignore the degree to which Althusser himself problematizes the concept of representation. Hirst's suggestions to replace this concept with that of signification or to concentrate more on the *means* of representation do not transcend Althusser's model in a significant way.

Perhaps a more vulnerable aspect of Althusser's theory from a deconstructive point of view is his insistence on an essential unity in ideology. This idea of unity figures prominently not only in his assertion that all ideologies in a society are unified under the ruling ideology, which is the ideology of the ruling class, but also in his willingness to posit an Ideology with a capital "I", which is a structural unity underlying all its manifestations, that is, all the lower-case ideologies. While explaining how he is justified in proposing "a theory of ideology *in general*," Althusser compares such a theory to Freud's theory of the unconscious and asserts that ideology is eternal in the same way as the unconscious is eternal according to Freud. Thus ideology is endowed with a structure and a functioning such as to make it a non-historical reality, i.e. an *omni-historical* reality, in the sense in which that structure and functioning are immutable, present in the same form throughout what we can call history... ("ISA," 161)

Althusser comes very close here to a Hegelian conception of history as the unfolding of an essence that always retains its underlying identity. Such a conception of history that is regulated by an essential unity is precisely the one that Derrida opposes as having been "in complicity with that philosophy of presence to which it was believed history could be opposed" ("Structure, Sign, and Play," 262).

However, it is also possible to see a similarity at this point between Althusser and Derrida. Just as Althusser is concerned with analyzing and exposing an underlying structure called ideology that appears in different forms under different historical circumstances, Derrida is engaged in a critical examination of our entire metaphysical heritage, "within which are produced... all the Western methods of analysis, explication, reading, or interpretation" (*Of Grammatology*, 46). The qualification "western" obviously does not invalidate my point, considering the scope of what that adjective denotes, both temporally and spatially.

According to Derrida, the philosophical tradition that he deconstructs is "the most powerful, the most extended, the most durable, the most systematic *discursive* formation of our 'culture'" (*Positions*, 28). Just as according to Althusser there is no conscious life outside ideology, according to Derrida, there is no discourse without metaphysics:

> *There is no sense* in doing without the concepts of metaphysics in order to attack metaphysics. We have no language--no syntax and no lexicon--which is alien to this history; we cannot utter a single destructive proposition which has not already slipped into the form, the logic, and the implicit postulation of precisely what it seeks to contest. ("Structure, Sign, and Play," 250)

But even if we accept that there is such a tradition and it is much more deeply engrained in our culture than anything that has opposed it so far, we cannot automatically assume that *all* our methods of analysis and interpretation have been produced within its limits. Derrida's insistence on the ubiquity of metaphysics is bound to trivialize it in the same way that Althusser's eagerness to unify and systematize ideology trivializes it by equating it with all of conscious life.

It is true that Derrida himself has provided the most important corrective to a view of tradition as an absolute unity by showing how it is dependent on the elements that challenge its authority; the very notion of "proper" meaning is metaphorical, the assertion of sameness requires the recognition of difference, etc. It would not be fair to accuse Derrida of assuming that the entire Western tradition is uniformly metaphysical in every respect and detail. But the force of his criticism still depends on the validity of his view that all the challenges to the dominant metaphysical assumptions have been contained and neutralized by the same metaphysics:

> It was within concepts inherited from metaphysics that Nietzsche, Freud, and Heidegger worked, for example. Since these concepts are not elements or atoms, and since they are taken from a syntax and a system, every particular borrowing drags along with it the whole of metaphysics. This is what allows these destroyers to destroy each other reciprocally. ("Structure, Sign, and Play," 251)

This passage is a particularly good example of Derrida's disposition to emphasize system and unity at the expense of change and conflict when it comes to portraying the philosophical tradition that he opposes. The claim that every particular borrowing from the language of metaphysics drags the entire system along with it is especially curious. Derrida is invoking the fact that words and concepts are context-dependent in order to turn around and say that they remain the same even in new contexts. Instead of acquiring different meanings through different usages, the terms of metaphysics remain attached to their initial contexts with a fatal inevitability.

Thus, no matter how rigorous and specific his analyses of particular texts, Derrida's dialogue is in the end always with the whole that is called Western metaphysics. Especially in the hands of his less inventive followers, this dialogue regularly turns into the tedious process of uncovering the same metaphysical secrets over and over again. On the other hand, when taken over by deconstructionists with more overtly political concerns, the same assumption of unity is translated into social terms. It is often taken for granted that metaphysical ideals of unmediated presence, natural truths, objective representation, etc. are the only means by which repressive social systems justify and maintain domination. But to believe this is not only to return to the notion that there are essential connections between philosophical positions and the political aims they serve. More importantly, it is to have an inaccurate view of social institutions. There is no reason to think that all forms of domination have to operate in the same way and by the same ideologies of centrism, purity, absolute truths, and hierarchies. Deconstruction's unification of metaphysics and its subsequent transfer of that unity to all mechanisms of social domination is very similar to the reliance of Althusser's and other theories of ideology on assumptions of unity and consensus. As John Thompson points out in relation to the concept of ideology in general,

> There is little evidence to suggest that certain values or beliefs are
> shared by all (or even most) members of modern industrial societies.
> On the contrary, it seems more likely that our societies, in so far as
> they are 'stable' social orders, are stabilized by virtue of the diversity
> of values and beliefs, and the proliferation of divisions between
> individuals and groups. The stability of our societies may depend,
> not so much upon a consensus concerning particular values and
> norms, but upon a lack of consensus at the very point where
> oppositional attitudes could be translated into political action.
> (*Studies in the Theory of Ideology*, 5)

In other words, the status quo could be preserved by encouraging difference as well as homogeneity or uniformity. Making metaphysics the only context in which a text can be related to questions of conflict and domination produces the same results as defining the ruling ideology as the only such context. In both cases, one is committed to a view of society that is centered on and operates by uniformity and consensus. Dissent from the norms is acknowledged, but often dismissed as secondary, as capable of ultimately being reintegrated into the system.

In the light of these observations, it is possible to conclude that both Althusser's theory of ideology and Derrida's conception of metaphysics are too abstract, unified, and comprehensive to be of much value in uncovering the links between specific social situations and specific discursive practices. The absoluteness of these conceptions also has the ironic consequence of defeating the very purpose of the theory that produces them. One starts out by defining ideology or metaphysics so that one can work out a strategy for opposing them, but the definition paradoxically contains the unopposability of what one had aimed to oppose. My view is that even if there is a level at which ideology or metaphysics (or whatever other name by which we choose to call the "enemy") becomes inescapable, that level of abstraction is not relevant to the analysis of discourse in relation to particular social conflicts.

The abstract and absolute nature of the system to be opposed in the theories of both Althusser and Derrida also causes their conceptions of opposition to be shallow in comparison to other aspects of their thinking. There is a lack of balance, a fundamental tension, between the complexity and rigor of Althusser's analysis of ideology and the philosophical superficiality of his scientism. The power of theory or science to transcend ideology, to know it and to remain outside it, is simply assumed and asserted rather than being argued. I see a similar lack of balance between Derrida's rigorous description of metaphysics, the ingenuity by which he traces its forms and transformations, and the euphoria he attaches to the terms by which he intends to displace it. Rorty is right in reminding us that

> The fact that language is a play of differences, as well as an instrument useful in acquiring knowledge, gives us no reason to think that words like *differance* and *trace* can do to, or for, philosophy what Heidegger failed to accomplish with his own magic words-- *Sein, Ereignis*, and so forth. ("Deconstruction and Circumvention," 3)

In fact, Derrida's typical strategy of *announcing* extensions in the meanings of familiar words, creating new ones, or *asserting* that his key words like "trace" or "differance" do not have meanings seems to me to show insufficient consideration for the phenomenon that he describes as textuality. In a social, historical context, the effects of the particular usages of language need not be in only one direction, that of indeterminacy, dissemination, overflowing of rationally defined limits, etc. The history of discourse also works in the direction of limiting the meanings and uses of certain terms perhaps more strictly than some of their users intend or wish. No matter how deliberately Derrida continues to transform his language, shifting the meanings of his own terms and inventing new ones, "general text," "differance," "hymen," "trace," etc. are today, in the context of a certain history of usages, meaningful *concepts*, immediately recognizable as parts of a specific philosophical project. Rorty is fully justified, for example, when he objects to Derrida's claim that "differance" is neither a word nor a concept. He is more faithful to an anti-essentialist view of language than Derrida when he explains:

> The first time that Derrida used that collocation of letters, it was, indeed, not a word, but only a misspelling. But around the third or fourth time he used it, it had *become* a word. All that it takes for a vocable or inscription to become a word, after all, is a place in a language game. . . . As to concepthood, we Wittgensteinian nominalists think that to have a concept is to be able to use a word. Any word that has a use automatically signifies a concept. It can't help doing so. ("Deconstruction and Circumvention," 18)

Indeed, to take Derrida too seriously when he announces that his key terms are meaningless by virtue of their opposition to the metaphysical "fullness of meaning" would be to fall into the error he himself denounced. With all his attention to the materiality of the signifier, his careful elaborations of the economies and the histories of words, Derrida has shown that intention or consciousness cannot serve as a stable locus, source or determinant of meaning. This is equally applicable to his own discourse. There is no reason to think that his intention *not* to limit the scope of a word such as "text" can accomplish what other philosophers' intentions to limit and purify their own words have not been able to accomplish. It is true that Derrida casts aside his own terms with almost the same rapidity with which he arranges for the emergence of new ones, but I doubt that such continuous house cleaning is sufficient resistance to metaphysical reappropriation. For one thing, his casting those terms aside does not take them out of circulation in deconstructionist writing in general. More importantly, the new terms he proposes cannot be understood or used independently of the terms they replace. There will always be a process of translation that will assign the new terms to the spaces occupied by the older magic words. In any case, Derrida's definition of metaphysics makes the construction of an anti-metaphysical language as problematic as Althusser's definition of ideology makes the construction of a "subjectless," scientific one. This in turn leaves the question of opposition unresolved.

It may seem that this question is not relevant to the issue of the ideological analysis of texts. One can, after all, diagnose and uncover something that one may not be able to oppose fully. However, the type of ideological analysis that I believe we need to develop does not consist of uncovering an ideology or a metaphysics that lies hidden in the text. Ideology is not such an independently existing entity that one can recognize and point at. It is a process by which a particular text places itself in the service of this or that social interest or viewpoint. Therefore, it can be analyzed only in the context of an alternative viewpoint representing alternative interests. As long as we recognize the untenability of the science/ideology dichotomy, that is, as long as we do not claim that our discourse is at some higher level than the one we are analyzing, our ability to construct a viewpoint that can oppose the one we are criticizing, our ability to speak in genuinely different terms becomes crucial. To the extent to which both Althusser and Derrida theorize the impossibility of such an opposition, their theories fail to provide useful frameworks for ideological criticism.

My aim in bringing together deconstruction and Althusser's theory of ideology is not to claim that they can be reduced to the same thing. There is indeed much to be deconstructed in the concept of ideology, and Derrida's methods are effective for this purpose. Deconstruction's attention to language, its suspicion of determinist models, its "textualization" of both text and context are valuable correctives to what has passed as ideological analysis before it. However, it would be wrong to ignore the points at which the two approaches converge, especially because these convergences give rise to remarkably similar strategies in confronting literary texts. This is the point I intend to illustrate in the next chapter by concentrating on the problem of according literary texts a special status with respect to ideology and metaphysics.

CHAPTER 3

LITERATURE AGAINST IDEOLOGY AND METAPHYSICS

When modern critics think they are demystifying literature, they are in fact being demystified by it; but since this necessarily occurs in the form of a crisis, they are blind to what takes place within themselves. At the moment that they claim to do away with literature, literature is everywhere; what they call anthropology, linguistics, psychoanalysis is nothing but literature reappearing, like the Hydra's head, in the very spot where it had supposedly been suppressed. The human mind will go through amazing feats of distortion to avoid facing "the nothingness of human matters." (Paul de Man, *Blindness and Insight*, 18)

Unjustifiably negative and absolute theoretical formulations of ideology have created several problems in the area of literary theory, and given rise to interesting responses to these problems. I pointed out earlier, while discussing the problems of the classical Marxist statements about ideology, that their inconsistencies became particularly striking when one considered such valued "ideological" institutions as science and art. In the case of science, as we have seen, the usual response to the problem of reconciling the contradiction between the illusory and class-dependent character of all ideological formations with the objective and universal character of scientific truth has been either to exclude all science from the arena of ideological battle between the classes or to use the term science to denote one's own view, claiming a status above ideologies by virtue of offering a critique of them. We have also seen that neither strategy is totally consistent and successful.

The case of art and literature is even more complicated. In general, it is more difficult to claim objective truth value for a literary text or a painting than for a scientific theory. Moreover, it is very difficult to envision painters, poets and novelists as producing their works in a kind of social vacuum, independently of their personal beliefs, political interests, unconscious wishes, etc., the way scientific institutions are often assumed to have made it possible for a scientist to work in her laboratory. There is hardly any way to avoid seeing art and literature as being ideological through and through. However, the conception of ideology being as negative and absolute as it is, as soon as one characterizes art as being ideological, one is faced with the question of how any expression of a "false consciousness" or any representation that serves to perpetuate repressive social relations can have positive aesthetic or cognitive value.

There is a tradition of working around this problem. It begins with Marx and Engels, and continues in most Marxist criticism up to our day, although it gets increasingly more complex and refined. Even more interestingly, this strategy, which I will call "saving the text," is not confined to the tradition of Marxist criticism. It forms one more link between ideological and deconstructionist analyses of literary texts. Before going on to speculate as to the reasons behind this link, however, I will explain what I mean by the strategy of saving the text, and some of the different forms it takes.

According to Marx, and especially Engels, realism was the greatest virtue in art. Just as materialism was opposed to ideology in philosophy, realism was opposed to ideology in the realm of art. An artistically faithful and complete representation of reality in a work of literature, for example, meant the transcendence of ideology in the sense of false consciousness and class prejudices. Realism, which according to Engels, was "the truthful reproduction of typical characters under typical circumstances" (*Art and Literature*, 114), implied, for the author, the ability to rise beyond his feelings and prejudices and to depict reality without distorting it according to his own class-bound subjectivity. Thus Balzac's greatness inhered not only in his having drawn a truthful picture of the French society of his time, but also in his having done this in spite of his own political sympathies, in spite of his own ideology. He had shown the inevitability of the bourgeoisie's success despite the fact that he himself was a Legitimist and emotionally tied to the collapsing aristocracy:

That Balzac thus was compelled to go against his own class sympathies and political prejudices, that he *saw* the necessity of the downfall of his favorite nobles, and described them as people deserving no better fate; and that he *saw* the real men of the future where, for the time being, they alone were to be found--that I consider one of the grandest features of old Balzac. (*Art and Literature*, 116)

In other words, Balzac's text triumphed over his ideology, perhaps without his having been fully conscious of this fact. Lenin's praise of Tolstoy for being the mirror of the Russian peasants in spite of his romantic, aristocratic ideals and delusions about the peasantry and about social relations in general, as well as Lukacs' much more sophisticated analyses of the masterpieces of nineteenth century realism continue this tradition to a great extent.

Such a solution to the problem is appealing for a number of reasons. If, through realism, art and especially literature can transcend its necessarily ideological character and become a form of knowledge, the work's value does not depend on the ideology of the individual author, his or her class origins, or the specific content of the work. There is no justification for demanding that literature be "committed," that it glorify certain values and condemn others, or that it dedicate itself to the portrayal of prescribed characters and situations. Engels makes this attitude quite explicit:

> I am far from finding fault with your not having written a point blank socialist novel, a "Tendenz-roman" as we Germans call it, to glorify the social and political views of the author. That is not at all what I mean. The more the opinions of the author remain hidden, the better for the work of art. (*Art and Literature*, 115)

It is easy to see that Engels' views about aesthetic value follow quite naturally from the theory of ideology developed in *German Ideology*. If ideology is an inverted picture of reality resulting from the subject's socially conditioned inability to perceive the outside world as it is, the transcendence of ideology is simply the perception of reality as it is, which art is able to bring about by being a faithful *reflection*. The questions that are not answered are, how this true reflection--realism--is achieved, and how it is recognized as having been achieved. There is no need to go into all the complexities, the changing conventions and the different senses of realism as a mode of artistic representation in order to see that this particular aesthetics of reflection rests more on assumptions than on theoretical analysis. The important thing is to observe how a strictly negative definition of ideology makes it necessary to invest art and literature with "trans-ideological" powers.

Certain features of this move are characteristic, and they also figure in later, more rigorously theoretical accounts of art's triumph over ideology, especially in theories of literary production. First, since the most natural and immediate locus of the ideological sources of a text is the individual author herself, she, as an empirical, historical being, has to be cancelled out, so to speak, by her text. The ideology of the author, regardless of whether it is in accord or in conflict with the representation of social reality achieved by the text, is not a significant factor in this achievement. In principle, Balzac's text would not have been any different if he had politically and emotionally been on the side of the rising bourgeoisie instead of the collapsing aristocracy. The power of his realism would have prevented him from writing a "Tendenz-roman," from glorifying the members of the bourgeoisie. Although this seems to be a rather commonsensical approach, especially since new criticism has already trained us well not to put any stock in authorial intentions, we must not totally lose sight of the fact that such blatant lack of correlation between the author as a concrete individual and the author as artist is problematic.

Second, it is interesting to note that the power of art to reflect reality and thus to transcend, at least the artist's ideology, is simply assumed rather than argued. Similar claims are not made for philosophy, historiography, religion or economics, at least not with equal confidence and enthusiasm. Although any text can be interpreted to have meanings not intended by the author or to represent realities that an author would, for ideological reasons, like to portray differently, it is not very often that one sees a philosopher, for example, being praised for not letting her ideas about social justice or injustice contaminate her philosophy of law. In fact if one could find a discrepancy between her pronounced views on one area and elements of her philosophical analysis on the other, that would simply be viewed as an inconsistency, not a source of greatness. On the other hand, a scientist *could* be praised for making a discovery that would help disprove the Christian account of creation in spite of his own Christian fundamentalist beliefs. Literature and science, then, both seem to have a special accord with reality so that simply by being faithful to the the natures of these discourses, the scientist or the novelist can transcend ideology.

A third characteristic of this approach is that while attempting to give a function and value to art as a whole, it necessarily leads to valorizing one type of art and denying authenticity to others. When realism is seen as the solution to the problem of ideology, it becomes the ultimate and only goal of artistic creation. Of course, concepts like realism can be defined in terms broad enough that they could include almost any work of art. But such an inclusiveness would probably trivialize a writer's accomplishment in having transcended ideology. In practice, the critics who follow in Engels' footsteps tend to canonize certain authors or periods, having definite and rather restrictive notions of what realism in art is or ought to be. Lukacs is a case in point.

As the concept of ideology gets more refined, so does the account of how it can be transcended in or through literature. Just as Engels' pronouncements on the relationship between ideology and realism started an entire tradition of criticism intent upon showing the triumph of the text over the author's ideology, Althusser's theory of ideology and his comments about art and literature served as a foundation for theories of how literature dismantles ideology in the very act of giving form and expression to it. Althusser himself was rather reluctant to see art as belonging fully to the realm of ideology. In a letter to André Dapré he said, "I do not rank real art among the ideologies, although art does have a quite particular and specific relationship with ideology" (*Lenin and Philosophy*, 221). The qualifier "real" in front of the word art here is certainly not accidental. But what exactly is this specific relationship that art has with ideology? Althusser explains it in the following terms:

> Art (I mean authentic art, not works of an average or mediocre level) does not give us a *knowledge* in the *strict sense*, it therefore does not replace knowledge (in the modern sense: scientific knowledge), but what it gives us does nevertheless maintain a certain *specific relationship* with knowledge. This relationship is not one of identity but one of difference. . . . What art makes us *see*, and therefore gives to us in the form of "*seeing*," "*perceiving*," and "*feeling*" (which is not the form of *knowing*) is the *ideology* from which it is born, in which it bathes, from which it detaches itself as art, and to which it *alludes*. (*Lenin and Philosophy*, 222)

This thesis brings into sharp focus the tendencies that I pointed out as existing in rather vague forms in the case of the reflectionist aesthetics of classical Marxism. The distinction between real, authentic works of art and those of an average or mediocre level is made clearly and emphatically, and tied directly to the relationship between the work of art and ideology. The claim that art constitutes a special mode of discourse having a special relation to ideology is equally clear. In fact, it is made in terms that are strongly reminiscent of a Kantian aesthetics, relegating art to the level of feelings and perceptions, although for Althusser, art still has some sort of connection with knowledge.

The most important difference between Althusser's account of art's relation to ideology and that of Engels and his followers is that for Althusser the ideology in question is no longer simply the ideology of the individual artist. Instead we have Althusser's more abstract and impersonal notion of ideology as a form of representation. Accordingly, there is no question of protecting the work of art from the intrusion of ideology. Art is born from ideology, bathes in it. However, it also alludes to it, and detaches itself from it. How can this detachment be accomplished?

A detailed answer to this question is provided by a follower of Althusser's in the field of literary theory, Pierre Macherey. According to Macherey, "it is in the significant *silences* of a text, in its gaps and absences, that the presence of ideology can be most positively felt," and "we always eventually find, at the edge of the text, the language of ideology, momentarily hidden, but eloquent by its very absence" (*A Theory of Literary Production*, 60). What for Althusser is given to us by the text in the form of feelings and allusions is, according to Macherey, made eloquent by gaps, silences, and absence. The vagueness and almost mystical tone in the language of each theorist is remarkable. Ideology is present in literature either in an unknowable, unstatable form, or simply in its absence. Again, according to Macherey,

> What is important in the work is what it does not say. This is not the same as the careless notation "what it refuses to say," although that would in itself be interesting . . . But rather than this, what the work cannot say is important because there the elaboration of the journey is acted out, in a sort of journey to silence. (86)

In both Althusser and Macherey the ideology of the author is replaced by what we might call the ideology of the text. However, the ideology of the text is not at all an aspect or an effect of the text. It is clearly referred to as existing before the text, giving birth and setting limits to it, but at the same time being exposed by it. It is not clear in what form the specific ideology being exposed by a text pre-exists it. Since ideology is itself a representation, it would seem that it exists either in the author's mind or as another text (in the broadest sense of the word). In either case, the literary text is secondary, derivative. It is the result of a transformation in which an already formed and present ideology is given a specifically literary form, and exposed in the process. Macherey is quite explicit in this regard:

> The writer is only the apparent author of the ideology contained in his work; this ideology is in fact constituted independently of him. It is encountered in his work, just as he himself encountered it in life. (115)

The general thrust of this hypothesis is not unusual or objectionable. No matter how we define ideology, it is reasonable to think that it is not created afresh within the bounds of every specific social "utterance," be it a literary text or a law. There is certainly an ideological background in the most general sense that makes these utterances and their interpretation possible. However, to say that an ideology is first formed outside the work (encountered in life), and then simply *contained* in it is to endorse an idealist concept of ideology. Instead of a constantly shifting and active discourse, ideology emerges as an entity, created once and for all, and then packaged in different containers.

In any case, defining the "literariness" of literature through its special relationship to ideology and then reducing this relationship to a mute signalling by the text of another text that is hidden on its fringes or in its interstices creates several problems. First, we might well ask why such ideological "subtexts" should be found exclusively in literary or artistic texts. Terry Eagleton, who, at least in his earlier writings, subscribed to the same Althusserian formula, offers a possible answer to this question when he says in *Marxism and Literary Criticism* that

> It is by giving ideology a determinate form, fixing it within certain fictional limits, that art is able to distance itself from it, thus revealing to us the limits of that ideology. In doing this, . . . art contributes to our deliverance from the ideological illusion. (19)

But the emphasis on form is hardly sufficient to set art and literature apart from other ideological practices. If ideology can be transcended only by being given a definite form, such formalized ideological systems as religion should be as liberating as art. But I may be equivocating on the term "form." What Eagleton probably has in mind is not simply that any definite form will expose its ideological basis, but that art makes ideology more accessible and thus criticizable, by making it concrete. Still, if it is the concrete experience that is portrayed in art that reveals the limitations of ideology, then why should not every individual be able to achieve the same liberation in the context of his own concrete experience? And, to return to Macherey, if it is through gaps and silences that the text liberates, it is hard to imagine any text, whether artistic or non-artistic, without such gaps and silences.

That Macherey, like Althusser and others before him, simply assumes that literature has a power to demystify ideology without demonstrating literature's difference from other types of discourse which are not credited with the same power is evident in his description of how the so-called demystification is accomplished:

> Even though ideology itself always sounds solid, copious, it begins to speak of its *own absences* because of its presence in the novel, its visible and determinate form. By means of the text it becomes possible to escape from the domain of spontaneous ideology, to escape from the false consciousness of self, of history, of time. The text constructs a determinate image of the ideological, revealing it as

> an object rather than living it from within as though it were an inner conscience; the text explores ideology . . . , puts it to the test of the written word, the test of that watchful gaze in which all subjectivity is *captured*, crystallised in objective form. The spontaneous ideology in which men live . . . is not simply reflected by the mirror of the book; ideology is broken, and turned inside out in so far as it is transformed in the text from being a state of consciousness. (132-33)

Here, despite the apparent complexity of the process described, the entire argument in defense of literature rests on a rather simple fact: that it is written. The written word can turn ideology inside out because it crystallises it in a definite, objective form. Even if we were to accept this valorization of writing without question, the separation of literature from other types of writing would remain unjustified.

Moreover, making literariness or artistic function dependent on the ability to reveal the workings of ideology through gaps and silences raises several questions about the practice of ideological analysis. We would be trivializing this idea if we took it to mean that the text never states its ideological premises directly, as a series of assertions. There might indeed be several explicit ideological proclamations within a literary text, but part of the process of interpretation consists of making decisions about the status of such proclamations, about whether they are to be taken at face value or as ironic, whether they reflect a character's views or the author's, etc. Thus, to the extent that the ideological elements of a literary text are never directly available, never simply there independently of the interpretation of the entire text, we do in fact articulate gaps and silences in the process of ideological analysis. But surely, this is in no way peculiar to the question of the text and its ideology. Articulating gaps and silences in this sense *is* the process of interpretation. The identification of any theme or metaphor, the establishment of genre, the perception of irony are all part of this process in which the reader makes inferences that are motivated but not spelled out by the text.

On the other hand, if we interpret Macherey's formulation strictly and conclude that it is *only* through what the text does not, cannot, say that it reveals the ideology which gave birth to it, we will have some difficulty establishing the limits of what is not said, and accounting for the significance of what actually is said. Since any text is one complex utterance among infinitely many possible ones, there are infinitely many things that it either chooses not to say or perhaps cannot say. Obviously, any of these possibilities would not be as good as the other in defining the ideological limits of the text. Any reader of Mailer's *An American Dream* would probably agree that what it does not say about women is more significant than what it does not say about the threat of nuclear war--precisely because of what it does say about women. This is probably a way of getting at what Macherey means, rather than an argument against him. I do not aim to caricature his thesis by implying that he does not see any connection between the elements of a specific text and its particular ideological background. But the point is that when we thus think of "what a text cannot say" as what one arrives at through interpretation of textual clues, it is hard to see how this sort of ideological interpretation is intrinsically different from interpretation in general, including the interpretation of religious, legal systems, and so on, or why literary texts are particularly amenable to it.

Thus, the gaps and silences of the text are in fact produced by a reading that has to take authorial intentions, literary and generic conventions, social contexts, and a number of other textual features into account. Given the complexity of these factors and the forms of interaction between them, we cannot say that what we arrive at through their interpretation is an already formulated or observable ideology that the text has simply made tangible, that it has mutely pointed at. In fact, we do not arrive at an ideology at all, in Macherey's fixed and global sense. We arrive at an account of the ways in which the text is implicated in relationships of power, domination, and struggle. Articulating this implication involves an analysis of the text as a particular utterance under specific conditions of production and reception. But Macherey, like Althusser before him, theorizes the notion of ideology to such a point of abstraction and absoluteness that it becomes necessary to accord a special status to any discourse that one does not want to see as being utterly dominated by ideology. This is what I call "saving the text" while performing an ideological analysis of it.

It is with respect to this rescue operation that the similarity between Althusser's and Macherey's ideology on the one hand and deconstructionists' metaphysics on the other reemerges. In both cases, an all pervasive, more or less unconscious system with its own vocabulary, history, and illusions is exposed and its limits overflown by the materiality of the text.

This is not to attribute to Derrida the idealized concept of literature that Macherey seems to have. Although analyses of literary texts have been important in his demonstration of the subversion of metaphysics by the phenomenon of textuality, Derrida explicitly rejects the notion that there is an inherently "anti-metaphysical" form of writing called literature:

> The irreducibility of writing and, let us say, the subversion of logocentrism are announced better than elsewhere, today, in a certain determined form of "literary" practice. But you can very well understand why I would write this word between quotation marks, and what equivocality must be brought into play. This new practice

supposes a break with what has tied the history of the literary arts to the history of metaphysics. (*Positions*, 11)

Indeed, one of the trademarks of deconstruction has been this keeping of literature and other terms in quotation marks, this rejection of essential boundaries between different discourses. Moreover, Derrida's conception of text is different from Macherey's. For all his emphasis on writing, he is still adamantly critical of interpretations of his theory that would limit the reference of "text" to the written word.

Significantly, his most direct statements to this effect have been in rather overtly political contexts. For example, in *Positions* it was as part of an interview in which deconstruction's relationship to Marxism was persistently interrogated that he expressed his vexation at his leftist critics' failure to understand that the general text was not limited to writings on the page (59-60). In the course of a more recent debate about his characterization of apartheid in South Africa he made the same point more emphatically:

> It is precisely for strategic reasons . . . that I found it necessary to recast the concept of text by generalizing it almost without limit, in any case without present or perceptible limit, without any limit that is. That is why there is nothing "beyond the text." . . . That is why South Africa and apartheid are, like you and me, part of this general text, which is not to say that it can be read the way one reads a book. . . . Not only, then, do I not go "beyond the text," in the new sense of the word text, but the strategic reevaluation of the concept of text allows me to bring together in a more consistent fashion, in the most consistent fashion possible, theoretico-philosophical necessities with the "practical," political, and other necessities of what is called deconstruction. ("But, beyond. . . ," 168)

Thus, expanding the meaning of the word "text" is, for Derrida, a strategic necessity in both philosophical and political senses. It is also his response to the accusations that he sees the world as consisting solely of what is written about it, that he obliterates the nonlinguistic contexts of discourse by textualizing everything. Accordingly, we should be careful not to implicate Derrida in the rather arbitrary operation of "saving the text" by equating text with the written word, or with literature, which, to him, are only special cases of textuality.

But we should also keep in mind that the uses of deconstructionist terminology and strategies are not regulated by Derrida's definitions and intentions. As I argued earlier, his redefinition of the term "text" does not erase the meaning this term had before his intervention, and even the more politically minded among his followers often oscillate between different senses of the word. For example, in his introduction to a volume of essays entitled *Displacement* that aims to illustrate "the cultural and ideological as well as the belletristic implications of deconstruction," Mark Krupnik writes that as a result of deconstruction's analyses, "the new subject of literary study includes society, and culture, and sexuality, and the unconscious, all considered as texts" (3). But if society, culture, sexuality, and the unconscious are texts in the sense in which everything else is a text, in the sense that they are relational and not present in themselves, I do not see why the recognition of such textuality should make them objects of literary study any more than objects of sociological, psychological, historical, and other types of inquiry. This reasoning reveals that the term "textuality" is still used in a way that is closer to its "literal" meaning than deconstructionists are willing to admit.

Moreover, Derrida's redefinition of text and his warnings against thinking the history of literature outside the history of metaphysics are not his only interventions into the field of literary criticism. At the same time that he questions the boundaries that separate literature from other types of discourse, Derrida's critique of Western philosophy depends on a fundamental distinction between philosophy and literature. Perhaps a more accurate way of expressing this is to say that his deconstruction of philosophy depends on a distinction between the philosophical and the literary uses of language. In the inverted form of the hierarchy, the literary becomes the name of a kind of writing that incorporates the awareness of its rhetorical status while philosophy remains mystified by its own dream of transcending that rhetoricity.

It has often been claimed that this privileging of the literary has been a main factor in Derrida's popularity among literary critics. Christopher Norris observes, for example, that

> Clearly there are pressing institutional motives for this readiness among literary critics to accept the broader drift of Derrida's arguments. It is agreeable to be told, after all, --and on good philosophical authority--that criticism is not just a poor relation of philosophy but possesses the rhetorical means to dismantle philosophy's claims to truth. ("Some Versions of Rhetoric. . .," 193-94)

It is true that Derrida's privileging of the literary might be only a heuristic device for him. Literature in his definition is a deconstructive force within discourse rather than a fixed body of writing. But in the hands of deconstructionist literary critics this heuristic definition becomes a new way of attributing deconstructive powers to literary texts in the narrower, more conventional sense. Paul de Man, for example, remarks that

> The statement about language, that sign and meaning can never coincide, is what is precisely taken for granted in the kind of language we call literary. Literature, unlike everyday language, begins on the far side of this knowledge; it is the only form of language free from the fallacy of unmediated expression. (*Blindness and Insight*, 17)

I do not see how we can read this statement without taking "literature" as referring to a certain body of texts conventionally considered the objects of literary study rather than as a deconstructive force, a version of "differance" operating in language in general. De Man refers to the literary as a "kind of language," not as a property of it, and rigidly distinguishes it from "everyday language."

I believe that this attitude is not due to a simple misinterpretation of Derrida's position by critics who are eager to increase the importance of their own profession. It is rather a continuation of the tendency in deconstruction to counter a metaphysics portrayed in absolute terms by invoking magic words that will expose its limits somewhat automatically. Literature thus becomes another part of the chain that contains such concepts as "differance," "trace," etc.

Macherey clearly expresses the view that exposing ideology is not a task performed by the reader or the critic, but an almost automatic function of the text itself when he says:

> Implicitly, the work contributes to an exposure of ideology, or at least to a definition of it; thus the absurdity of all attempts to "demystify" literary works, which are defined precisely by their enterprise of demystification. (133)

These are almost exactly the same terms in which Hillis Miller explains why texts cannot really be deconstructed since they deconstruct themselves; they are, in fact, defined precisely by their enterprise of self-deconstruction:

> My account of deconstruction has been misleading, however, if it has suggested that the dismantling is performed from the outside by the critic on a piece of language which remains innocently mystified about its own status. This is by no means the case. The "unreadability" (if there is such a word) of a text is more than an experience of unease in the reader, the result of his failure to be able to reduce the text to a homogeneous reading. It is also always thematized in the text itself in the form of metalinguistic statements.

These may take many forms. The text performs on itself the act of deconstruction without any help from the critic. ("Deconstructing the Deconstructors," 31)

If there is any ambiguity here about what the term "text" denotes, it is clarified by several more explicit statements by other deconstructionist critics. Barbara Johnson, for example, maintains that

> The difference between literature and criticism consists perhaps only in the fact that criticism is more likely to be blind to the way in which its own critical difference from itself makes it, in the final analysis, literary. (*The Critical Difference*, 12)

This formulation is particularly revealing because it shows how the expansion of the meaning of the term "literary" does not prevent the privileging of literature in the narrow sense. If the literary is language's difference from itself, literature is the type of writing that is aware of that difference, that is thus more literary, more deconstructive than other discourses. Paul de Man can thus say that "poetic writing is the most advanced and the most refined mode of deconstruction" (*Allegories of Reading*, 17).

To a great extent, these views boil down to the assumption that what liberates literature from the mystification attached to other types of discourse is its acknowledgement that it does not "speak the truth," that it is a linguistic construct, not a sign for some sort of presence or reality. Rorty claims, for example, that

> For the textualists, the literary artist's awareness that he is making rather than finding, and more specifically the ironic modernist's awareness that he is responding to texts rather than things, puts him one up on the scientist. ("Textualism . . .," 156)

But these claims rest on a simplified conception of fictionality and rhetoric. The fact that a novel, for example, is fictional, that its individual statements do not claim to be verifiable or falsifiable by empirical data, is hastily assumed to mean that literature does not intend to be about reality, that it has no claim to truth. Similarly, the foregrounding of language and rhetoric in literature is implausibly taken as proof that literature ultimately amounts to a happy demonstration of its own rhetoricity, not aspiring to be about anything other than itself.

Those who make these assumptions forget what they themselves have ingeniously demonstrated on several occasions: that any text can be read as referring to its own mode of discourse, whether it is "literary" or not. If in philosophy, history, or religion, language does not seem to incorporate the awareness of its rhetorical status, as literature is assumed to have done all along, it is because the "readers" of these discourses take the truth claims they contain seriously, if only to refute them later. All deconstructionists, above all Derrida, show as evidence of philosophy's unfounded claim to truth, presence, authenticity, or proper language, the statements of the philosophers to that end. Then, by calling attention to the textuality of philosophical discourse, by showing the very concepts of presence and authenticity to be dependent on absence and repetition, by exposing the metaphorical status of philosophy's condemnation of metaphor, they "reduce" philosophy to where literature was to begin with.

But what if we were equally attentive to the proclamations within and surrounding what are known as literary texts? What if, when they announced their far from modest intentions to probe the depths of human nature or existence, to create something more real than reality, not only to reveal, but even to violate and to change truth, we took novelists or poets seriously; that is, if we did not assume that they were merely jesting in accordance with some narrative or rhetorical convention, and accepted their claims at face value? What if, when literature acknowledged metaphor and claimed it as its own, it were not renouncing the adequacy of its language to truth, but boldly enlisting metaphor as a powerful instrument in the search for truth? Then literature would not be "one up" on the scientist or the philosopher. It would not self-deconstruct as gracefully as one had hoped, just as it does not dismantle ideology as automatically as Macherey seems to think.

Gerald Graff's criticism in *Poetic Statement and Critical Dogma* of the New Critics' denial of all types of propositional content and referential meaning in literature is also valid against the deconstructionist overemphasis on rhetoricity and self-referentiality in literature. Graff shows, through careful readings of individual poems as well as logical arguments that indicate the inconsistencies of "organicist" and "non-cognitivist" positions, that defining literariness as an antithesis to rational discourse does not do justice to our experience of literature. The features of poetry that the New Critics valued most highly, features like archetypal content, synthesis of attitudes, dramatization of conflicts, tensions generated by a complex verbal context, etc. "cannot flourish in isolation from conceptual assertion and predication, from 'opinion as to matters of fact, knowledge, belief'" (171). The same is true of the literary features that deconstructionists value. We cannot perceive or formulate the deconstructive tensions in a text without taking it as a structure of conceptual assertions, and we cannot even define rhetoricity in isolation from any content which rhetoric conveys.

If literature really does make truth claims, then "saving the text" through deconstruction is a paradoxical operation. In order for literature to become the privileged term in the hierarchical opposition between philosophy and literature, it must first forsake its claims to any kind of truth. In order for the essentialist distinction between literary and other types of discourse to be questioned, literature paradoxically has to be treated as if it were indeed intrinsically different from them.

This leads to parallel paradoxes in deconstructionist statements about the authority and the function of the critic. On the one hand, the critic seems to possess the means to go beyond the surface structures of a text to reveal underlying patterns of language or textuality, and to turn the text against the metaphysical intentions which produced it. He also seems to gain unlimited freedom in his interpretations of texts, since he is no longer bound with the restrictions that apply to modes of interpretation in which those intentions are seen as constraints upon the meanings of a text. Since his own discourse refuses to see the literary text as an "object" of analysis in the sense of having a determinate and stable identity, it becomes as non-referential as literature itself, and thus a form of poetic writing. In *Criticism in the Wilderness*, Geoffrey Hartman claims, for example, that there are no real boundaries between criticism and literature, that criticism itself is literary. Hillis Miller expresses a similar view in "Critic As Host," showing how literary texts and commentaries on them are equally parasitic on other texts, and how they are simultaneously hosts and parasites for each other.

On the other hand, the insistence on the self-deconstruction of the text, on its power to demystify the critic who thought that he was the demystifier, seems to make the critic rather superfluous. Since the literary text is cut off from the author's intentions and does not embody some kind of truth, there are no secrets about it to which the critic can have special access. Roland Barthes expresses this view most emphatically when, after announcing the "death of the author" as a source of meaning in the text, he remarks that

> there is no surprise in the fact that, historically, the reign of the Author has also been that of the Critic, nor again in the fact that criticism (be it new) is today undermined along with the Author. (*Image-Music-Text*, 147)

But only slightly earlier, in *Critical Essays*, Barthes had also written that once the privileged position of the author as the source of textual meaning had been rejected, once criticism stopped aiming to reconstruct meanings that were supposed to be already in the text, the critic would gain a new power:

> Thus begins, at the heart of the critical work, the dialogue of two histories and two subjectivities, the author's and the critic's. But this dialogue is egoistically shifted toward the present: criticism is not an

> homage to the truth of the past or to the truth of "others"--it is a construction of the intelligibility of our own time. (*Critical Essays*, 260)

The interesting thing about this struggle, which, as Frank Lentricchia has pointed out in *After the New Criticism* (211), can hardly be called a dialogue, is that the same indeterminacy of meaning, which was supposed to undermine the critic along with the author, is here described as a fact that empowers criticism, that liberates the critic from being subservient to the author and the past. Stanley Fish takes the same approach when he claims that rejecting objective criteria in interpretation saves the critic from being "the humble servant of texts whose glories exist independently of anything he might do" (*Is There a Text In This Class?*, 368)

There is a similar ambiguity about the status of critical discourse in Macherey. While he speaks of the "absurdity of all attempts to 'demystify' literary works, which are defined precisely by their enterprise of demystification" (133), he also employs a strikingly "deconstructionist" language to assert that an author's knowledge "is implicit, blind to its own scope and origin" (117), and to draw a rather rigid distinction between literary and critical discourses:

> Thus, between the writer and the critic, an irreducible difference must be posited right from the beginning: not the difference between two points of view on the same object, but the exclusion separating two forms of discourse that have nothing in common. The work that the author wrote is not precisely the work that is explicated by the critic. Let us say, provisionally, that the critic, employing a new language, brings out a *difference* within the work by demonstrating that it is *other than it is*. (7)

This issue of the "power struggles" between authors and critics, authors and readers, critics and readers, etc. has been the subject of many discussions of the politics of criticism implied by ideological and deconstructionist analyses. For example, in "The Politics of Literary Criticism," Evan Watkins complains that the division of literature into a "surface structure" and an underlying "deep structure" "participates in the division of labor by appropriating literature into a surface which the author 'intended' . . . and an underlying pattern available only to the critic-analyst" (*The Question of Textuality*, 32). He goes on to say,

> It is because of this intense and often painful drama of social interaction that I want to conceive of the critical act as political

through and through and not only when it is put into relation with other and more obviously political behavior. (37)

I do not agree that the discussion of the relative authorities of writers, readers, and critics is the description of a "drama of social interaction." The ease with which the same theories of literature can lead to radically different views on this matter, even in the writings of a single critic like Barthes, shows that a politics of critical discourse in this sense is bound to remain a pseudo-politics. I believe that the authority of a critic is established and supported in institutional terms, by a network of social relationships including those that regulate universities and publishers, the economical and cultural factors that determine different social groups' access (or lack of it) to texts as writers and readers, etc. As such, this authority is an object of sociological analysis. This is not to say that it is irrelevant to or beyond the reach of literary criticism, but it cannot be settled by a discussion of the properties of literary texts.

However, Watkins does have a point about the ease with which both deconstructionist and other types of ideological analyses gain a certain freedom from demonstrating their hypotheses by asserting beforehand that they are dealing with latent structures independent of individual intentions. The way in which both Althusser's and Derrida's conceptions of discourse always cancel out the speaker, the individual who makes the specific utterance, does present a problem for textual analysis. Within such a framework, every text becomes only a particular manifestation of a larger, more abstract entity like ideology or language. The critic thus addresses the abstract entity, disregarding to a great extent that the discourses she is analyzing are produced by conscious subjects. I find John Thompson's reminder of this point particularly helpful:

> It is important to stress that, in the case of interpreting ideology, there is an additional consideration which comes into play. For the interpretations generated by the depth-hermeneutical method are about an object domain which consists, among other things, of subjects capable of reflection; and if their claim to truth is to be sustained, then these interpretations would have to be justif*iable* in the eyes of the subjects about whom they are made. (*Studies in the Theory of Ideology*, 14-15)

In other words, the claim to be revealing a latent ideology or metaphysics does not constitute an automatic claim to truth. Ideological analysis needs to be freed from the rhetoric of clinical detachment and mastery which often permeates such operations as deconstruction, demystification, and the like. It is important to remember that its very definition and purpose compels it to be a dialogue between equals. Neither theories of ideology like Althusser's nor deconstructionist analyses have so far been able to support such a dialogue. They have both been too ready to "save" texts while asserting the "blindnesses" of their authors and critics.

CHAPTER 4

DECONSTRUCTING THE SUBJECT

I see, practically and theoretically, the estranging consequences of the general assumption--as active in modernist literature as in theoretical linguistics and structuralist Marxism--that the systems of human signs are generated within the systems themselves and that to think otherwise is a humanist error. There is then a paradox: that these systems, as systematic analysis reveals them, have great explanatory power, but that the form and language of their explanations are at a quite exceptional distance from the lives and relationships they adress, so that what is reaching furthest into our common life has the mode of a stranger, even the profession of a stranger. (Raymond Williams, *Writing in Society*, 224)

As such, history is not human, because it pertains strictly to the order of language; it is not natural, for the same reason; it is not phenomenal, in the sense that no cognition, no knowledge about man, can be derived from a history which as such is purely a linguistic complication; and it is not really temporal either, because the structure that animates it is not a temporal structure. (Paul De Man, "The Task of the Translator," 92)

It is easy to see from the analysis in the preceding chapter that the emphasis on writing as an impersonal act and the discounting of authorial intention are important components of the claims made about the anti-ideological or self-deconstructing characteristics of literary texts. Beginning with Engels' endorsement of a realism faithful to truth despite the author's personal ideological commitments, continuing in the psychoanalytical overtones of Macherey's attention to what a text cannot admit about itself, and achieving a fully systematic form in the deconstructionist view of rhetoricity as capable of turning every utterance against its apparent or intended meaning, there is a deeply rooted refusal to grant authors or individual speakers an autonomy that would give them control over their own discursive practices. Although this refusal is connected to the process of "saving the text" where literature is shown to defy the ideological and metaphysical intentions that produce it, it would be wrong to see such a refusal as merely a maneuver to attribute subversive functions to literary texts. The critique of the intentional theory of meaning is in fact an essential element of a general eradication of the individual subject in post-structuralist philosophy and criticism. Understanding the basis for this eradication is important because it has implications for the ideological analysis of discourse on several levels.

The deconstruction of the subject as a philosophical category develops from structuralism and Saussurian linguistics. Ferdinand de Saussure maintains in *The Course in General Linguistics* that language is a system (langue) of arbitrary signs which underlies and makes possible each meaningful utterance (parole). The objects of linguistic study are the contrasts between signs and the possibilities of combination through which signs create larger units of meaning. These relations and possibilities are determined independently of the intentions of individual speakers. "The distinguishing characteristic of the sign--but the one that is least apparent at first sight--is that in some way it always eludes the individual or social will" (*Course*, 17). Although Saussure's text is open to significantly different interpretations, there is no question that his emphasis on the determining role of system runs counter to the humanist celebration of imagination and free consciousness. Frank Lentricchia points out, along these lines, that

> in its affirmation of a wholly relational and differential view of discourse as system, Saussure's thought recollects Nietzsche in that it constitutes a rigorous antihumanism at least in intention (pace Jacques Derrida). (*After the New Criticism*, 115).

Structuralist applications of this "antihumanistic" linguistics as a model for all cultural systems have led to many different versions of the idea that individuals can be viewed as intersections of and supports for these systems rather than their producers. While asserting the universal validity of his anthropological investigation of myths, Levi Strauss, for example, explains:

> I therefore claim to show, not how men think in myths, but how myths operate in men's minds without their being aware of the fact. . . . it would perhaps be better to go still further and disregard the

thinking subject completely, proceed as if the thinking process were taking place in myths. (*The Raw and the Cooked*, 12)

In *Of Grammatology* and other places Derrida has criticized the systematizing and universalist assumptions of structuralism as well as its failure to acknowledge the "structurality of structures" by which the very notion of system gets caught up in a play of differences and loses the stability that most structuralists attribute to it. He continues, however, the dismantling of the notion of an autonomous and conscious subject which has already been started by structuralist analyses of language and culture, and which we saw as being central to Althusser's theory of ideology.

Derrida claims that the notion of a conscious subject as the starting point of its own discourse is enmeshed in the metaphysical desire for a nonderived primary ground, a self-identical entity prior to the textuality of language and culture. He maintains that such an origin is not possible because the subject of an utterance is a subject by virtue of the fact that it is making the utterance, that it is a "speaking" subject. But if this is true, it is as completely governed by the rule of "differance" as the words in the utterance:

> What was it that Saussure in particular reminded us of? That "language [which consists only of differences] is not a function of the speaking subject." This implies that the subject (self-identical or even conscious of self-identity, self-conscious) is inscribed in the language, that he is a "function" of the language. He becomes a speaking subject only by conforming his speech--even in the aforesaid "creation," even in the aforesaid "transgression"--to the system of linguistic prescriptions. ("Differance," 145)

It is possible to challenge Derrida's interpretation of Saussure as having said that language consists only of differences. Robert Scholes, for example, says that the deconstructionist emphasis on the role of difference in Saussure's theory is not entirely warranted (*Textual Power*, 19). Even though Saussure did say that words, phonemes, and other linguistic elements signified by virtue of their differences rather than their intrinsic properties, he did not conclude that other factors, such as reference, could be left completely out of the understanding of signification. Nevertheless, we can still grant Derrida the point that the speaking subject has to conform to linguistic prescriptions, and thus cannot be the pure origin of the meaning of its utterance.

At this level of analysis, Derrida'a critique of the subject is not a consequence of, but simply identical to his critique of what he considers the metaphysical conception of meaning. He claims that this conception depends on positing a subject which dominates the scene of its utterance through the self-presence of its intentions. The privileging of the spoken word, for example, depends on, or derives from, the notion that the speaker, at the moment of the utterance, constitutes a starting point of unity between word and intention. As he hears himself speak, the stability of his meaning is guaranteed by the proximity of the external, material sign, the word, to the internal, ideal concept, the signified. It is only after the word is heard, repeated, inscribed, and thus detached from the originating intention that the self-presence of meaning is corrupted and stands in need of recovery. Derrida calls this theory of a self-present meaning logocentrism because it posits speech, logic, reason, or God's word as an originary and regulating center. Logocentrism places writing in a binary opposition to speech. In its spatial and temporal distance from the original speaker, writing becomes the name of meaning's absence, mediacy, difference from itself. Because it characterizes writing and thus difference as being secondary to the absolute proximity of voice and being, logocentrism is the metaphysics of phonetic writing.

Derrida counters this logocentrism, not by simply valorizing writing, but by reversing the hierarchy between speech and writing, and displacing the opposition between them. He shows that speech is dependent on writing in the sense that the elements of difference, repeatability, and mediation that are associated with writing are what make all signification, including speech, possible. In *Of Grammatology* he explains that

> Writing is the dissimulation of the natural, primary, and immediate presence of sense to the soul within the logos. Its violence *befalls* the soul as unconsciousness. Deconstructing this tradition will therefore not consist of reversing it, of making writing innocent. Rather of showing why the violence of writing does not befall an innocent language. There is an originary violence of writing because language is first, in a sense I shall gradually reveal, writing. "Usurpation" has always already begun. The sense of the right side appears in a mythological effect of return. (37)

"The immediate presence of sense to the soul" is an impossibility because sense emerges only through the mediation of a mark or a sign, and the very identity of a sign is constituted by its "iterability," that is, by its participation in a code. For a sign to be a sign, it must be repeatable in other contexts. Even when used for the first time, it functions by its dissociability from an individual subject and under the condition that the code is prior to the intention. If intention depends for its very existence on a code that the subject has neither created nor can control, it and the consciousness presumed to be its source are always already written, devoid of a reality and an identity more stable than language.

There is one basic objection that can be raised against this "linguistic" critique of the "speaking subject." Because it depends on the critique of intentional meaning, its validity is limited by the epistemological adequacy of Derrida's deconstruction of intentionality. If we accept that the iterability and the conventional nature of language necessarily forbid assigning intentions a significant role in the production of meaning, we also have to accept that the subject, insofar as it is defined as the source of these intentions, drops out of consideration.

But Derrida's arguments are far from having demonstrated that we can do without the notion of intentionality. John Searle, for example, responds to Derrida's exclusive emphasis on iterability by pointing out that iterability is not something that disrupts intentions to mean, but simply a minimal condition for language to exist:

> As Derrida is aware, any linguistic element written or spoken, indeed any rule-governed element in any system of representation at all must be repeatable, otherwise the rules would have no scope of application. ("Reiterating the Differences," 199)

When viewed in this way, which I think is the only reasonable way to view it, iterability cannot be an obstacle to intentionality any more than the mere existence of language can be seen as an obstacle against it. In this sense, Derrida's thesis that writing and speech are not fundamentally different, that the repeatability clasically attributed to writing is also an element in verbal communication, is true but trivial. It is a necessary consequence of the fact that both speech and writing are uses of language. If Derrida had demonstrated that writing could be read without any need for construing the intentions of the author, and then shown writing in this sense to be an element in all language, the reversal of the hierarchy between writing and speech would indeed result in a refutation of intentional meaning. But as Searle points out, the simple fact that a written text can be read in the absence of its original author or addressee does not show that we can interpret the text without knowing that it was an intentional utterance and without understanding each meaningful sentence as a realization of a corresponding intention to mean. Intention can still be viewed as determining meaning to the extent that it forms the link between a rule-governed system and the understanding of particular utterances. Thus, according to Searle,

> iterability. . . is not as Derrida seems to think something in conflict with the intentionality of linguistic acts, spoken or written, it is the

necessary presupposition of the forms which that intentionality takes. ("Reiterating the Differences," 208)

The same point can easily be made about the conventionality of language. The fact that linguistic conventions precede individual subjects and are beyond their control does not diminish the role of intentions in the ways these conventions are applied. Knapp and Michaels express this point well when they ask:

> Why should the claim that language is essentially conventional, even if it were true, undermine the possibility of saying what one means? Why should the need to follow the conventions compromise intention if the intention is an intention to follow those conventions? ("Against Theory 2," 62)

If the fact that intentions could not be realized without the conventional linguistic system made the role of the speaking subject secondary enough that it became a mere function of the system, we could simply reverse the emphasis and follow the same logic to say that the system was a function of the subject since it would remain only a potentiality for meaning without the particular intentional utterances of individual speakers. This indicates that there are no absolute dichotomies between system and utterance, convention and intention, language and subject.

These arguments do not by themselves prove that individual subjects' intentions unambiguously determine the meanings of their utterances in all contexts or that they are directly available as criteria for the validity of interpretations. They do show, however, that the transition from the "impersonality" of linguistic systems to the notion that human subjects themselves are mere functions of these systems is not as ineluctable as it appears. By emphasizing conventions, iterability, and the risk of failure in the communication of intended meanings, Derrida's deconstructions demonstrate that individual subjects do not have absolute control over their uses of language. They do not demonstrate that they have no control. However, most deconstructionist analyses proceed as though this lack of absolutes showed us something very significant about the human condition.

In "On Translation," Paul de Man provides a striking example of this strategy while he builds on Walter Benjamin's views about language and translation to use translation as a model for the dissociation between language and human intentions. He illustrates this point with an example originally provided by Benjamin. In order to show the discrepancy between "dire" and "vouloir-dire," he examines the relationship between the German word "Brot" and the French word "pain." The translation from the French into the German, for example, would involve using the word "Brot" to name what in French is named by "pain." But the translation reveals a "fundamental discrepancy between the intent to name Brot and the word 'Brot' itself in its materiality," by setting in motion an entire chain of connotations, cultural associations and "dissimulations" that are beyond the control of both the original author and the translator:

> If you hear "Brot" in this context of Hölderlin, who is so often mentioned in this text, I hear *Brot und Wein* necessarily, which is the great Hölderlin text that is very much present in this--which in French becomes *Pain et vin*. "Pain et vin" is what you get for free in a restaurant, in a cheap restaurant where it is still included, so "pain et vin" has very different connotations from those things--I now hear in "Brot" "bastard." This upsets the stability of the quotidian. . . . What I mean is upset by the way in which I mean--the way in which it is "pain," the phoneme, the term "pain," which has its set of connotations which take you in a completely different direction. (87)

The same point could be made, of course, without bringing up the question of translation at all. It is obviously just as impossible to apprehend all the connotations of a word while speaking or writing within one language as it is to control all the shifts that will occur during the transition to another language. In any case, this upsetting of meaning by the mechanisms of meaning themselves, this lack of control on the part of the language user, constitutes, for de Man, the inhumanity of language:

> The way in which I can try to mean is dependent upon linguistic properties that are not only not made by me, because I depend on the language as it exists for the devices which I will be using, it is as such not made by us as historical beings, it is perhaps not even made by humans at all. (87)

It would be easy to argue in moral, philosophical, or political terms with the notion that language was not made by people as historical beings. But that would involve quarelling with an overstatement that does not necessarily need to be taken seriously as a theoretical principle of deconstruction. I chose this example because it illustrates in a very clear way how the deconstructionist objection to the notions of human control over language and history, individual autonomy, and thus the very notion of the subject, often depends on the construal of the concepts of humanity, autonomy, and subjecthood in very absolute ways. It assumes that if these concepts cannot be defined in unproblematic terms at the level of the single utterance, they are always and inherently problematic, regardless of the contexts in which they occur, and the purposes for which they are used.

My response to this attack on absolutes is the same as the one Robert Scholes voices in a recent essay on "Deconstruction and Communication" where he argues persuasively that Derrida's theory of language does not have consequences upon which a new understanding of communication could be built:

> I do not see how we get from this discussion of absolutes to any practical conclusions. If everything in our world is impure, insofar as we know anything about it, this means that purity is not a concept that we can use, except in a relative way: more or less pure, more or less impure. (288)

Similarly, the question of the speaker's control over the meaning of his utterance is one of degree, not of absolute presence or absence. It is true that words have unintended connotations and they can be interpreted in contexts not controlled by the original speaker or author. But this does not obliterate the distinction between the word "Brot" and the word "bastard" in any specific context. De Man's ability to hear one in the other does not result inevitably from the materiality of language. It results from his concentration on the material sound qualities of these words outside the circumstances of any particular intentional utterance. To do this is not to be talking about meaning any more. To think that such a procedure tells us something important about the nature of language is to assume that deconstruction has demonstrated the complete irrelevance of human intentions to the process of interpretation.

Just as de Man exaggerates the epistemological significance of Derrida's deconstruction of the subject's autonomy, those who think that this deconstruction results in dissolving the metaphysical opposition between individuals and social systems exaggerate its ideological significance. According to this view, the ideal of an autonomous, self-present subject serves to sustain the division between the public and the private, creating the illusion that there can be a pure self outside the social realities and discourses that engender it. The displacement of the centrality of the subject in language helps destroy that illusion by revealing individual subjects to be functions of larger relational systems. Michael Ryan explains, for example, that

> the deconstructive displacement of the centrality of the cogito is the opening of that personal instance onto a differential, institutional, and historical text that constitutes it without being subject to its identitarian form. (*Marxism and Deconstruction*, 220)

In general terms it is true that any type of ideological analysis is concerned with placing individuals in larger systems, situating them in conditions beyond their absolute control. The deconstructionist emphasis on the role of conventions, codes, and other non-intentional, public aspects of language is consistent with such an aim. But a specifically deconstructionist view of language is neither necessary nor sufficient for an awareness of the social nature of discourse. The example of de Man's reasoning shows that the lack of individual control over language does not necessarily imply that language has to be understood as being social in any significant sense of the term. Just as a critique of the absolutely determinate intentional meaning has little to say about the actual practice of communication, seeing subjects as functions of linguistic systems teaches little about the political aspects of language use. To the extent that all subjects are dependent on liguistic systems for the their very existence as subjects, control over these systems or lack of it is not a political issue. It becomes political only when one begins to consider whether and how such control is achieved in different degrees by different social groups. For example, the feminist criticism of sexism in language is based on the claim that women have not had as powerful an influence on the language they speak as men. If we followed Paul de Man's standards in measuring human control over language, it would be very hard to see this difference as significant. Men cannot put a stop to chains of connotations any more than women. Devices of meaning upset men's intentions to mean as much as they upset women's. Debunking the myth of autonomy does not lead to a discovery of specific limitations on it. In this sense, it would not make much difference if Paul de Man, after his demonstration of the connotative powers of language, concluded not that language was inhuman, but that it was social. This would not amount to much more than saying that everything was social. De Man's position here is not simply politically useless, but so counter-intuitive in its implications that it points up the theoretical inadequacy of his viewpoint.

I said above that the weaknesses of Derrida's deconstruction of intentionality constituted one possible objection to his "linguistic" critique of the "speaking subject." The second objection is simply that it is a "linguistic" critique of the "speaking subject." Even if we grant that language can, in principle, function independently of individuals' intentions, this does not undermine all conceptions of subjective autonomy and identity. In "Differance," after his Saussurian critique of the subject, Derrida anticipates one objection of this kind. What, he asks, if we say that although the subject has to obey the linguistic structure at the moment of speaking, although it has to enter the system of differences in order to signify, we can conceive of a presence of the subject before speech, "a subject's self presence in a silent and intuitive consciousness"? But such a question supposes that

> prior to signs and outside them, and excluding every trace and differance, something such as consciousness is possible. It supposes, moreover, that, even before the distribution of signs in space and in the world, consciousness can gather itself up in its own presence. (146-47)

In other words, when we define the subject as being inside the linguistic system, we have to accept its place as a function instead of an origin or presence. If we try to conceive of it as being outside language and in consciousness, we have to subscribe to a version of idealism in which thoughts can exist without being embodied in anything material such as a signifier. It is still legitimate to wonder if, as Derrida evidently assumes, these two cases really exhaust all the alternatives. Why should opposing the linguistic determination of the subject require positing its "self presence in a silent and intuitive consciousness"? But before we pursue this question, we should understand the other objections that Derrida has against the notion of pure consciousness.

Derrida sees the question of consciousness as being connected not only to the desire for an autonomous, "prelinguistic" subject, but also, and not independently from the issue of language, to the desire to posit a human identity that would transcend its temporal, historical determinations, and collect its various modes of being in a unified center, assuring continuity and self-sameness over change and contradiction. In "The Ends of Man," for example, he cites Hegel's philosophy to illustrate the complicity between the idea of consciousness and the denial, through reappropriation, of time:

> Truth is here the presence or presentation of essence as *Gewesenheit*, of *Wesen* as having-been. Consciousness is the truth of man to the extent that man appears to himself in consciousness in his Being-past, in his to-have-been, in his past surpassed and conserved, retained, interiorized (*erinnert*) and *relevé* . (*The Margins of Philosophy*, 121)

Here the emphasis is on unity rather than autonomy and control. In rejecting the Hegelian notion of the subject, Derrida wants to situate difference not as a boundary that defines a subject by its uniqueness, its difference from other subjects, but as a force within individual identity, as the subject's difference from itself. This is why he attaches a special importance to Freud's notion of the unconscious, and discusses it, in *Writing and Difference*, as the intrusion of writing into the psyche.

Because the unconscious is not the simple opposite of consciousness and separable from it, because it exists only as the distortion of conscious thought processes, it has no permanence that would enable thought to recover and negate it. It disturbs the unity of the subject not by simply dividing it, but by dividing it without being a part of it:

> The unconscious is not, as we know, a hidden, virtual, and potential self-presence. It is differed--which no doubt means that it is woven out of differences, but also that it sends out, that it delegates, representatives or proxies; but there is no chance that the mandating subject "exists" somewhere, that it is present or is "itself," and still less chance that it will become conscious. In this sense, contrary to the terms of an old debate, strongly symptomatic of the metaphysical investments it has always assumed, the "unconscious" can no more be classed as a "thing" than as anything else; it is no more of a thing than an implicit or masked consciousness. ("Differance," 152)

I do not believe we can argue with the idea that there can be no such pure and autonomous entity as consciousness existing outside any form of materiality and preserving its sameness in the face of change and contradiction. We can, however, ask whether consciousness need be defined in this way.

In an essay entitled "Wittgenstein on Consciousness and Language," Charles Altieri argues that it need not. Using Wittgenstein's implicit definition of consciousness as "a way of relating to actions we learn to perform" (1403), Altieri argues that Derrida's deconstructions depend on unnecessarily construing consciousness as a pure representational force, "a mysterious inner process with its own rules and energies" (1402). Even though Derrida is right in showing the inner contradictions of such a view of consciousness, his critique does not invalidate all notions of conscious identity and selfhood. If, as Altieri proposes, we follow Wittgenstein and see thinking as "not a separate activity but a way of proceeding in other more specific activities," if we see it as "a style or mode of acting, not the imposition of a separate set of forms" (1402), we can view consciousness in terms that are very different from the Hegelian ideal that Derrida deconstructs. Instead of a "special subject of thought which one can seek by self-reflection" (1403), consciousness becomes the name of the various forms of involvement of human beings in the world. It becomes a process by which individuals define themselves through their actions. From this perspective, individual identity does not have to be located in a unified consciousness, and Derrida's deconstruction of this unity is not as important as it seems.

However, those who would like to use the deconstruction of the subject for the purposes of ideological analysis point out that Derrida's questioning of the unity and identity of the subject is important because these properties attributed to the subject by metaphysics form the basis of individual subjects' accountability in the face of higher forms of authority. The essential identities of individual subjects justify their *subjection* to the existing norms that regulate their social lives.

Derrida provides an example for this perspective on the notion of a unified subject in his analysis of Blanchot's fiction in "Living On." According to Derrida, Blanchot's novels and stories problematize the notion of a unified subject by refusing to fulfill the expectations traditionally associated with story, narrator, and character. Blanchot uses several techniques to obliterate the distinctions between the end and beginning of a work; the narrator, the author and the characters; the frame of the story and the referential frame outside it; and so on. The recounting of events is continually interrupted and caught up in paradoxes not only by a lack of temporal or other kind of order in the story, but also by the lack of continuity in the "subject" who is alleged to have experienced or perceived these events and who is required to narrate them. Thus in *L'arret de mort*, for example,

> [The story's] end, which comes before the end, does not respond to the request of the authorities, the authorities who demand an *author*, an *I* capable of organizing a narrative sequence, of remembering and telling the truth: "exactly what happened," "recounting facts that he remembers," in other words saying "I" (I am the same as the one to whom these things happened, and so on, and thereby assuring the unity or identity of narratee or reader, and so on). Such is the demand for the story, for narrative, the demand that society, the law that governs literary and artistic works, medicine, the police, and so forth, claim to constitute. (98)

The unified subject is in this sense constituted by legal, medical, and psychiatric discourses as both the condition and the effect of their power.

Once again, Derrida's notion of metaphysics shows a striking similarity to Althusser's theory of ideology. The constitution of the subject is accomplished in and by what Derrida calls metaphysics in the same way as it is accomplished by Althusser's ideology. Even the choice of examples brings out this similarity. Just as Derrida's example from Blanchot's text concentrates on a subject being questioned by the authorities, Althusser's model for the constitution of the subject refers to an individual on the street being "interpellated" by a policeman. In the "theoretical scene" that Althusser constructs to illustrate how ideology transforms individuals into subjects, a policeman hails an individual: "Hey, you there!" When the hailed individual turns around, "by this mere one-hundred-and-eighty-degree physical conversion, he becomes a *subject*"

(*Lenin and Philosophy*, 174). He becomes a subject because "he has recognized that the hail was 'really' addressed to him, and that it was really him who was hailed (and not someone else)" (174). In other words, the identity of a subject is furnished by a discourse which demands a certain compliance to the rules. When the individual recognizes himself as the one being hailed, he simultaneously recognizes the authority over himself of the one who hails, or rather the practice of hailing, of interpellation. "The existence of ideology and the hailing or interpellation of individuals as subjects are one and the same thing" (175). In a similar way, Derrida's "society," "law," "medicine," and "police" demand a story which would assure the unity and the identity of the subject. If Blanchot's narrator had said "I" in this sense, he would have recognized authority the way Althusser's individual does by turning around to respond to the policeman's hailing. In both cases subjecthood is a submission to a demand from the outside and not a matter of individual agency.

That subjects are constructed within discourses and institutions is a very important insight of poststructuralist philosophy. Both Derrida's and Althusser's examples dramatize this insight in an interesting way. But the dramatization seems to me to present too simplistic a picture of the overall process. In both cases, the demand for a coherent subjectivity comes from an outside authority itself construed as single and unified. Althusser's policeman stands for ideology as a whole. Derrida's "society," "law," "medicine," and "police" act in unision to make the same demand. Althusser's individual is passively and completely converted into a subject through recognizing himself in a monistically defined ideology. Derrida's fictional individual resists by refusing to be the unified subject that the authorities expect him to be. In neither story is there room for the plurality of discourses and practices through which subjectivities are constructed in the real world.

Thus, even if at this very abstract, symbolic level, simply discarding the notions of subjective unity and identity seems to have an ideological value, this value is limited, once again, by the epistemological inadequacy of a very monistic view of society and ideology on the one hand, and of radical scepticism about individual identity on the other hand. Even if we agree with Derrida's critique of a unified and unifying consciousness as the source of an illusionary, metaphysical notion of individual identity, we are left with the question of how individuals do in fact say "I," how they do in fact have a sense of subjective continuity despite change and the heterogeneity of their experiences, and how they do form a sense of identity that can challenge and resist dominant discourses. Because Derrida's deconstructions do not offer answers to these questions, his views about human subjects are, as Raymond Williams points out about all "antihumanist" explanations, "at a quite exceptional distance from the lives and relationships they address" (*Writing and Society*, 224).

68 *Deconstructing the Subject*

We can see this even more clearly in Derrida's critique of the Cartesian conception of the subject and in the alleged ideological applications of this critique.

The notion of subject, according to Derrida and other poststructuralists, is in complicity with a certain epistemology of representation. In "Sending: On Representation" Derrida cites the distinction made by Heidegger between the pre-Cartesian notion of what-is as presence, and the modern, Cartesian conception of what-is as consisting in "an object (*Gegenstand*) brought before man, fixed, stopped, available for the human subject who would possess a representation of it." The very etymology of the word *repraesentatio*, according to Heidegger, relates the real "to the self who represents it and in this way [forces] it back to the self as a determining field." The human subject thus becomes the "domain and the measure of objects as representations, its own representations" (307). In this sense, the concept of the subject rests not only on a distinction between it and a world of objects, but also on its power to dominate the object world through representation.

Those who believe that this critique of the "subject" has ideological implications claim that the idea of a sovereign subject is used by those in power to define, and thus to a certain extent to create, what is human in their own image. According to this view, the Cartesian dualism between mind and matter reflects and justifies the desire of a dominant bourgeois class to separate the subjects or agents of domination from its objects or victims. While rationality, freedom and autonomy are systematically associated with the concepts of "man" and "subjectivity," the same attributes are denied to everything that is culturally defined by its "otherness" to "man": most notably nature, women, children, "inferior" races, and the insane. The essential isolation of the modern subject is thus a cultural assumption maintained by political and economical structures out of the need to objectify everything that those in power can know, exclude, and dominate in their role as subjects. Francis Baker claims that philosophical idealism and the positivism of bourgeois science join forces to this end:

> At the same time as bourgeois power rarefies the material in its search for the tranquil and tranquilizing ideal, --the fable of the ascertainment of its own domination--it also, as its other side, issues onto a positivism of the object. It must master the body of the world in practice at the same moment and within the same gesture and purposes as it de-realizes it in thought: not so much denying the world--which on the contrary, it strives to dominate--as opening up that powering and powered division between body and soul, object and subject, which is the principle of its sexuality, its epistemology and its representation, and which in the widest sense designs the

characteristic structures of the new culture. (*The Tremulous Private Body: Essays on Subjection*, 18)

The subject is in this sense the locus of power. It is not, as bourgeois philosophy seems to claim, an entity definable by its separability from the world of objects. It is a fantasy that grounds and disguises political power in epistemological terms. Consequently, deconstructing this epistemology effectively displaces the question of the subject from the realm of epistemology into that of politics.

One can claim, in this context, that even if deconstruction does not help much in the attempt to discern and challenge the inequalities between the degrees of autonomy different subjects have, simply challenging the authority of the sovereign subject would reveal the illusory nature of the culturally established oppositions between those who qualify as "real" subjects and those, who are, for some reason or another, seen as "less than" subjects. For example, in patriarchal discourses which privilege "man" as the model for the sovereign subject, women are displaced as "the others" who do not have the properties attributed to the "proper human being," the unified and self-present subject of metaphysics. When we recognize that these properties are in fact illusory, that there are no autonomous, authentic, unified subjects, we can have a basis for overturning the hierarchical oppositions between "man" and his "others." Just as phonocentrism can be countered by revealing writing to be an element already within speech, "phallocentrism," the discourse that takes the male subject as its center, can be countered by identifying the female element within all subjects. In this sense, femininity would be analogous to writing or textuality.

Derrida makes such an analogy in *Spurs: Nietzsche's Styles*. His reading of Nietzsche reverses Nietzsche's misogyny to reveal the "non-identity" of "woman" as a reason for affirmation rather than negation. As Gayatri Chakravorty Spivak explains in "Displacement and the Discourse of Woman," Nietzsche sees women as "impersonators" in an important sense. They do not have the same capacity as men to have authentic sexual experiences: "Finally--if one loved them . . . what comes of it inevitably? that they 'give themselves,' even when they--give themselves. The female is so artistic" (*The Gay Science*, 317). Spivak, in her reading of Nietzsche's statement, makes it quite clear why Derrida can easily turn the same statement into an affirmation of femininity:

> Women impersonate themselves as having an orgasm even at the time of orgasm. Within the historical understanding of women as incapable of orgasm, Nietzsche is arguing that impersonation is woman's only sexual pleasure. At the time of the greatest self-possession-cum-ecstasy, the woman is self-possessed enough to

organize a self-(re)presentation without an actual presence (of sexual pleasure) to re-present.("Displacement and the Discourse of Woman," 170)

Since, for Derrida, all "actual presences" are questionable, the "style" of the woman, the "representation" without presence, becomes exemplary:

> She writes (herself) [or (is) written--Elle (s')ecrit]. Style amounts to [or returns to (revient à) her. Rather: if style were (as for Freud the penis is "the normal prototype of the fetish") the man, writing would be woman. (*Spurs*, 56)

Thus Derrida turns Nietzsche's woman which is a "bad" model into a "good" model. Woman is like writing because "she plays dissimulation, ornament, lying, art, the artistic philosophy" (*Spurs*, 66). Spivak's article takes this "affirmation of woman" by Derrida as a point of departure to question Derrida's use of the notion of femininity in general. It is not necessary, however, to follow her entire reading of the many complicated reversals this notion undergoes in Derrida's writing to agree with her conclusion that "the woman who is the 'model' for deconstructive discourse remains a woman generalized and defined in terms of the faked orgasm and other varieties of denial" ("Discourse of Woman," 170). In his reversal of the hierarchy between "man" and "woman," Derrida repeats the patriarchal gesture, analyzed in detail by such authors as Simone de Beauvoir and Luce Irigeray, which accords the woman the status of "what is not man." In the process of her rise to become the "upper" term of the hierarchy, the woman loses her claim to sexual or any other kind of authenticity, turning into a force of division and fissure, another version of "differance," rather than a being in her own right. Here, we can apply to Derrida the observation that Tania Modleski makes in "Feminism and the Power of Interpretation" about Peggy Kamuf's and Jonathan Culler's deconstruction of the female reader: "although Kamuf and Culler want to destroy the concept of 'origin,' the attempt works best when 'woman' is the (vanishing) subject" (134).

Spivak concludes her analysis with the judgement that "even the strongest goodwill on Derrida's part cannot turn him quite free of the massive enclosure of the male appropriation of woman's voice" (190). I believe that the reason for this is not simply that this enclosure is indeed "massive," or that Derrida is, after all, a man. The inadequacy of Derrida's "feminism" in this case is exemplary of the inadequacy of the general deconstructionist method of overturning hierarchical oppositions. This, in turn, is connected to the overdependence of deconstruction's revisionary strategies on the terms, construed in the most absolute way, of what is being challenged. In order to make this clear, we should briefly spell out what this revisionary strategy is.

In "Differance," Derrida claims that all the binary oppositions upon which traditional, metaphysical discourse is built can be dismantled by showing that the poles of the opposition are not really pure and do not exist independently of each other. This does not make the opposition disappear. But because one term of the opposition is always privileged as the "real" thing and the other is seen as a derivation of it, showing the derivation, the "supplement" to be within the privileged term, showing that the privileged term depends for its existence on the exclusion of its opposite, undermines that privilege. In other words,

> We could thus take up all the coupled oppositions on which philosophy is constructed, and from which our language lives, not in order to see opposition vanish but to see the emergence of a necessity such that one of the terms appears as the differance of the other, the other as "differed" within the systematic ordering of the same (e.g. the intelligible as differing from the sensible, as sensible differed; the concept as differed-differing intuition, life as differing-differed matter; mind as differed-differing life; culture as differed-differing nature; and all the terms designating what is other than *physis--techne, nomos,* society, freedom, history, spirit, etc.--as physis differed or *physis* differing: *physis in differance*). (148)

We have already seen how Derrida applies this overturning to the logocentric opposition between writing and speech. His deconstruction of the subject in general, and the idealized masculine subject of "phallogocentrism" in particular, works in the same way. In very simple terms, to the male subject that says to the female, "you are not a subject because I am the center and you are outside it," Derrida says, "all subjects are inevitably decentered, and thus you also are woman." But in order for this answer to work, the woman needs to remain "more" decentered than the man, she has to be the figure of decenteredness itself.

We encountered the same problem in the preceding chapter when we discussed how deconstructionists claimed to overturn the hierarchy between literary and referential discourses. In order for the literary to be valorized and to be revealed as an essential element in all discourse, it had to forsake all claim to truth. Then, what exactly do we do to a hierarchichal opposition when we reverse it? And what would happen if we simply attempted to think and speak outside the frame of that opposition, without contaminating each term with its metaphysical opposite, simply defining it in a new context? Derrida finds this attempt futile, and even politically harmful:

> To deconstruct the opposition, first of all, is to overturn the hierarchy at a given moment. To overlook this phase of overturning is to forget the conflictual and subordinating structure of opposition. Therefore one might proceed too quickly to a *neutralization* that *in practice* would leave the previous field untouched, leaving one no hold on the previous opposition, thereby preventing any means of *intervening* in the field effectively. We know what always have been the *practical* (particularly *political*) effects of *immediately* jumping *beyond* oppositions, and of protests in the simple form of *neither* this *nor* that. (*Positions*, 41)

There are, then, mainly two alternatives: either we remain within the metaphysical opposition and "displace" it, or we jump beyond it and leave the "previous field untouched." The examples of "femininity" or "literature" show that simply overturning a hierarchy does not displace it sufficiently. How, then, can we go beyond the opposition without leaving the previous field untouched?

I believe that this question arises, or at least seems more problematic than it is, because "the previous field" is already defined as the only field, the only context in which the opposition has been formed and the only context in which it can or cannot be opposed. We have already seen this insistence in Derrida's notion of metaphysics in general. We see it again in its application to the notion of the subject. By not looking for contexts outside metaphysical philosophy or the law of patriarchy to situate the subject, Derrida, as Susan Handelman puts it, remains "in the line of the Jewish prodigal sons who try to perpetuate the law in its own transgressions," and "repeats the scripture he seeks to analyze" (*The Slayers of Moses*, 166).

It is not a coincidence, then, that the issue of the subject and the related concepts of identity, autonomy, and experience have been an area of major tension between deconstruction and feminist criticism, even its deconstructionist varieties. Women are understandably more sceptical than men about turning their claims to identity and subjecthood over to a project that does not seem to offer much more than a fragmented self irreducably decentered by the abstract forces of "textuality"; they have had much fewer opportunities to enjoy the privileges associated with subjecthood.

Feminist criticism developed out of a concern with "femaleness as the experience of a female subject" (Teresa de Lauretis, *Alice Doesn't*, 165). Speaking as female subjects, feminist critics challenged the distorted representation of women in the discourses of patriarchy, and they continue to do so. This challenge inevitably depends on a distinction between the reality of women's experiences and their representations. It also depends on the assumption that women have a particular authority over these experiences, that they can know and represent what their own experiences are. Deconstructionist perspectives on the construction of the subject and on the divided nature of consciousness have constituted an important reminder that we cannot assume a simple coincidence or continuity between female subjecthood and the biological condition of being a woman, between a pre-existing experience and its representation in discourse. However, they have made the quest of feminist criticism seem more paradoxical than it is by concentrating on a very limited notion of subjecthood defined within a very limited context, and often obliterating the distinctions between different types of claims to subjecthood. Deconstruction does not necessarily lead to an erasure of these claims, but it fails to provide the terms in which they can be dissociated from the paradoxes of language and consciousness.

Not only for the sake of feminist criticism, but for the ideological analysis of discourse and representation in general, we must find ways of situating the subject in the context of action and community, of seeing the questions of identity, autonomy, and experience as being defined and redefined through the political alternatives that emerge in the process of social change. For, as Teresa de Lauretis rightly points out, what is at stake is not the language-determined "speaking subject," but

> subjects who speak and listen, write and read, make and watch films, work and play, and so forth; who are, in short, concurrently and often contradictorily engaged in a plurality of heterogeneous experiences, practices, and discourse, where subjectivity and gender are constructed, anchored, and reproduced. (*Alice Doesn't*, 171-72)

The deconstruction of the "subject" takes place at a level of abstraction too far removed from these experiences and practices, and what it demonstrates is the "impurity," the ambiguity of this concept, not its invalidity. The example of Derrida's notion of "femininity" as an attempt to go beyond this "impure" notion of subjecthood shows that such attempts remain trapped in the oppositions they seek to transcend. Derrida himself sees this danger and concedes that the "*real* conditions" of women's struggles "often require the preservation (within longer or shorter phases) of metaphysical presuppositions that one must (and knows already that one must) question in a later phase--or another place" ("Choreographies," 70). In other words, he concedes that at what he calls a "*practical level*," the distinctions between male and female subjects, between degrees of "subjecthood," degrees of autonomy, have to be acknowledged and examined. Perhaps this shows that these distinctions are not mere "metaphysical presuppositions." It seems to me quite ironic that one should spend so much time and energy trying to invalidate distinctions one will nevertheless be compelled to continue using for "practical purposes." In any case, the deconstructionist objections to the abstract linguistic, idealist, or Cartesian notions of the "subject" do not provide either epistemological or ideological reasons for abandoning this concept altogether.

CHAPTER 5

CRITICISM AND COMMUNITIES

the [interpretive] strategies in question are not his [the reader's] in the sense that would make him an independent agent. Rather, they proceed not from him but from the interpretive community of which he is a member; they are, in effect, community property, and insofar as they at once enable and limit the operations of his consciousness, he is too. (Stanley Fish, *Is There a Text In This Class?*, 14)

the reader is without history, biography, psychology; he is simply that someone who holds together in a single field all the traces by which the written text is constituted. (Roland Barthes, "The Death of theAuthor," 148)

    Any critic interested in seeing literary texts not as isolated artifacts complete in themselves, but as participating in the relationships between human beings would be attracted to the notion of an interpretive community. This is not simply because it contains the word "community," but because it seems to promise an account of the link between interpretation and society. If this link could indeed be spelled out, it would help us see that texts are social not by virtue of some intrinsic properties that they have, or by virtue of simply "representing" social relationships, but that they become social entities in the process of being interpreted by individuals who are members of communities. A knowledge of how these communities are formed, how they define and change the objects of their interpretations, would thus be essential for examining the political aspects of reading. Since I concluded in the previous chapter that the deconstructionist treatment of the subject does not take adequate account of the notion of community, it will be useful to bring it in contact with a theory which bases not only the act of interpretation, but even the concept of the subject on that of community.

The notion of an interpretive community can be seen as part of important and more or less parallel developments in the philosophy of science and literary theory that have taken place during the last few decades. The works of such historians, philosophers, and critics as Thomas Kuhn, Paul Feyerabend, Richard Rorty, Stanley Fish, and David Bleich attempt to show the impossibility for philosophy or literary theory to occupy a neutral transcendental position from which principles about the limits and scope of knowledge in general can be established and objective grounds for deciding which representations are true can be provided. These accounts of science and literature stress the paradigmatic nature of all types of inquiry and the theory-laden character of all facts. They reject the image of knowledge as an increasingly more faithful representation of an objective state of affairs, whether that be nature, the real world, or a meaning encoded in a text. Adopting the view that there are no universal criteria for rational validation of hypotheses, and that scientists as well as critics change their views through persuasion rather than demonstration, they attack the Cartesian mind/body duality as the source of a bankrupt epistemological tradition aiming to rule on the legitimacy of the intellectual endeavors of the entire culture. According to this account, the definition of mind and matter as ontologically separate entities is the framework in which philosophers have so far tried to formulate the notions of the observational given and the truth of meaning, providing unshakable empirical grounds for knowledge. They propose that this project be abandoned, for knowledge needs no foundation, and there is no way to separate the empirical from the conceptual. Most of the authors sharing this perspective also claim that abandoning the search for an absolute, supra-historical and universal foundation of knowledge would result in a new awareness of communal activity and responsibility in the shaping of human knowledge.

To the extent to which all these views stress the social origins of knowledge, reject the positivist notion of pure observational facts, and reveal the significance of various community interests that bear on scientific and literary activities, they are of interest for a discussion of the politics of literature and literary criticism. However, they tend to attribute a crucial role to the society or community in the shaping of knowledge without having recourse to a theory of social change and without explaining what exactly makes up a community. Moreover, some of the epistemological claims that they make raise serious doubts about the possibility of ever developing a theory of social change, of identifying social formations as knowable entities, and explaining the process through which certain forms of viewing the world come to be preferred over others. This is a problem that leads to circularities and vagueness in the usages of such concepts as paradigm, incommensurability, and community. In order to illustrate this problem and discuss its implications for a discussion of the political aspects of literary study, I will consider Stanley Fish's theory of interpretive communities in some detail. This will necessitate a brief overview of Thomas Kuhn's work in the history of science, since most of the concepts that Fish implicitly relies on are explicitly defined and discussed by Kuhn.

In *The Structure of Scientific Revolutions* Kuhn defines scientific paradigms as "models from which spring particular coherent traditions of scientific research" (11). Normal science is conducted by scientists whose research is based on shared paradigms and who are committed to the same rules and standards for scientific practice, while revolutionary science comes about at those historical moments when an existing paradigm is declared invalid and a new one takes its place. This rejection of the reigning paradigm occurs only when an alternate candidate is already available. Moreover, every paradigm defines its own problems and the acceptable strategies for solving them.

The important thing about this description of scientific activity is that it does not picture scientists as being confronted with objective facts which can be observed independently of their theories, verifying or falsifying them. Data are so infused with theory that what a scientist observes is necessarily a function of his beliefs, professional goals, and other social and psychological factors. Truth in the sense of a correspondence between reality and our image of it cannot be a criterion for comparing different theories or explaining why scientists change paradigms, since there is no reality that is available to observation independently of theories and mental constructs. The absence of truths outside and above paradigms makes paradigms incommensurable, meaning they cannot be compared and evaluated according to fixed criteria of validity applicable to all of them.

With examples from the history of science Kuhn shows very convincingly that there is no need to believe in the hitherto sacred myth of science as the purest, most objective form of human knowledge, and the concept of paradigm works well in this context. Difficulties arise, however, once we accept his criticisms against the objectivist views of scientific activity, and take a closer look at the particulars of the process he is describing. First, in the way Kuhn uses it in this book, "paradigm" seems to be an infinitely expandable or compressible term. For example, in an essay titled "The Nature of a Paradigm" Margaret Masterman identifies twenty-two different senses in which Kuhn uses the word paradigm in *The Structure of Scientific Revolutions*. These senses, ranging from "a standard illustration" or a "type of instrumentation" to a "general epistemological viewpoint" or "something which defines a broad sweep of reality" are certainly not all inconsistent with each other, but this broadness of meaning clearly limits the applicability and the explanatory power of the term.

When later, in *The Essential Tension*, Kuhn addresses this problem, his tendency is to limit the domain of his theory severely by introducing the concept of a disciplinary matrix: "'disciplinary' because it is the common possession of the practitioners of a professional discipline and 'matrix' because it is composed of ordered elements of various sorts, each requiring further specification" (297). The most important constituents of a disciplinary matrix thus described are "symbolic generalizations, models, and exemplars." Whatever clarity this definition provides for the concept of paradigm, I find it disappointing in its limited scope. In Kuhn's account that follows this definition, the basic elements of a disciplinary matrix for a mathematician, for example, turn out to be nothing more than the mathematical symbols she learns to use, the preferred analogies that she employs, and the sample solutions to problems that textbooks provide her with. I do not doubt that these are important factors that shape a scientist's professional behavior, but I do not see how some of the truly significant characteristics that Kuhn attributed to paradigms, and that make his work as a historian of science revolutionary in many respects can be applied fruitfully to the concept of disciplinary matrices. In what significant sense, for example, are these matrices incommensurable with each other? It seems that each scientific discipline has its own matrix, but it would certainly be absurd to claim that mathematics and physics are incommensurable. Also, it is hard to imagine how this definition of a paradigm could be used for a sociological investigation of scientific practice. How, for example, would scientific symbols or textbook problems and solutions be related to the financial, ideological, religious concerns of the scientists?

The earlier, fuzzier notion of paradigm would lend itself more easily to sociological inquiry because its definition could be interpreted as including such concerns. Since Kuhn says that a paradigm "stands for the entire constellation of beliefs, values, techniques, and so on shared by the members of a given community" (*The Structure of Scientific Revolutions*, 175), we could conclude that these beliefs and values would provide a link between the scientific community and the larger society that includes it. But a disciplinary matrix is defined in much more exclusively technical and institutional terms. In this sense, it reflects the tendency in Kuhn to restrict the sociological aspects of science to a consideration of the structure and mechanisms of scientific institutions, neglecting the impact of the larger society on the theories and the applications of science.

In the area of literary studies Stanley Fish comes closest to employing the concept of disciplinary matrices without using either this term or "paradigm." Although he does see people as "products of social and cultural patterns of thought" (*Is There A Text In This Class?*, 332), the only patterns of thought that he refers to as shaping people's reactions to works of literature are those developed in institutions of higher education. The presence of these institutions with interpretive strategies for producing texts seems to be his only guarantee against irrationalism and intellectual anarchy in the study of responses to literature:

> It is the reader who "makes" literature. This sounds like the rankest subjectivism, but it is qualified almost immediately when the reader is identified not as a free agent, making literature in any old way, but as a member of a community whose assumptions about literature determine the kind of attention he pays and thus the kind of literature "he" "makes." (11)

Fish's reduction of the social character of literary response to "interpretive strategies" that exist prior to and independently of individual readers is analogous to Kuhn's reduction of the social determinants of scientific activity to "disciplinary matrices." In Fish's case, there is an especially marked emphasis on the *authority* of the interpretive community:

> At this point it looks as if the text is about to be dislodged as a center of authority in favor of the reader whose interpretive strategies make it; but I forestall this conclusion by arguing that the strategies in question are not his in the sense that would make him an independent agent. Rather, they proceed not from him but from the interpretive community of which he is a member; they are, in effect, community property, and insofar as they at once enable and limit the operations of his consciousness, he is too. (14)

The interpretive community thus emerges as the end, the dissolving point in the "struggle" between the reader and the text. It saves the critic from being "the humble servant of texts whose glories exist independently of anything he might do" (368), while at the same time, owing to its intersubjective status, "solipsism and relativism are removed as fears" (321).

Fish is very open about the fact that he is especially concerned with removing the fears his theory of interpretation might inspire. Since his model for criticism is one of persuasion rather than demonstration, he has to address these fears that the members of the literary community might have, and he has to persuade them that to believe in his theory is "in [their] own best interests" (369). He does so by assuring us that to see texts and facts as being constituted by interpretive strategies is not to declare all interpretations equally valid or to remove all constraints on reading:

> We have everything that we always had--texts, standards, norms, criteria of judgement, critical histories, and so on. We can convince others that they are wrong, argue that one interpretation is better than another, cite evidence in support of the interpretations we prefer; it is just that we do all these things within a set of institutional assumptions that can themselves become the objects of dispute. This in turn means that while we still have all the things we had before (texts, standards, norms, criteria of judgement), we do not always have them in the same form. (367)

This emphasis on the *theoretical expediency* of the concept goes hand in hand with a lack of interest in examining interpretive communities in themselves, asking how and why they are formed, how and why they change, and in exploring the functions of these communities that go beyond sanctioning certain procedures of reading.

According to Fish, "an interpretive community is at once objective, in the sense that it is the result of an agreement, and subjective, in the sense that only those who are party to that agreement (and who therefore constitute it) will be able to recognize it" (178-79). Thus, the possibility of agreement and disagreement depends upon a prior agreement upon relevant concerns and the acceptable means of negotiating them. According to Fish, as according to Kuhn, a paradigm is what the members of a community share and a community consists of people who share a paradigm.

But as soon as we define a community as a group of people sharing a paradigm, the concept of community begins to suffer from the vagueness of the concept of paradigm. If, for example, we take a paradigm to mean a worldview, "something which defines a broad sweep of reality," how should we identify the community that corresponds to it? It can, of course, be said that communities are formed in different sizes, structures, and various relationships with each other, and thus also come in different levels of paradigmatic homogeneity. Adherents of a certain critical school, for example, would form a community that would itself be part of an academic community, that in its turn could belong to an even larger, less homogeneous structure. There would be several overlaps between different communities, and their configurations would change even within short periods of time according to different circumstances. Fish seems to have such a picture in mind when he explains that

> Interpretive communities grow larger and decline, and individuals move from one to another; thus, while the alignments are not

permanent, they are always there, providing just enough stability for the interpretive battles to go on, and just enough shift and slippage to assure that they will never be settled. (172)

When viewed in this way, however, community becomes a rather trivial concept. To say that there are different communities in this sense is the same as saying that individuals participate in a number of different groups and institutions that are relevant to their concerns, needs, desires, etc. I cannot argue with this statement, but I do not see how the recognition of this fact sheds any new light on the issue of paradigms, how they change, and how they can or cannot be compared with each other. If we used the term in this loose sense, we would not be able to avoid the relativism and intellectual anarchy that Fish fears so much. For every point of view, a community that would authorize it could be found or defined, and from there it would be an easy step to claim that different points of view are incommensurable.

The more restricted meaning in which Fish and Kuhn often use the term "community" has exactly the opposite disadvantage: it is too restrictive. It reduces the concept either to a formal institution such as the scientific or the literary profession, or to the simple, in many ways inscrutable fact of agreement. In the first case we achieve a clear-cut definition of community, but it becomes very difficult to explain the existence of radical disagreement within such institutions. More importantly, it is very counterintuitive to say that an individual can be "community property," that the "operations of his consciousness" are "enabled and limited" solely by the strategies of the community, when the community in question is a single formal institution such as the literary profession. Every individual participates in many different communities, and every individual acquires strategies for interpreting facts and sign systems through participation in communities. In this sense, every community is an interpretive community. There is no reason to think that the strategies developed in an institution of higher education to interpret what are constituted as literary texts will be the only determinants in the act of interpretation, even if one is acting under the assumption that the text is literary. Thus the presence of shared assumptions in a literary institution does not necessarily explain all agreements or disagreements between members of this institution.

In the second case, when we reduce the concept of community to that of agreement, it loses its explanatory power by being derived from what it was supposed to have made possible. Fish makes this paradox explicit:

> If everyone is continually executing interpretive strategies and in that act constituting texts, intentions, speakers, and authors, how can any one of us know whether or not he is a member of the same

> interpretive community as any other of us? The answer is that he can't, since any evidence brought forward to support the claim would itself be an interpretation. . . . The only "proof" of membership is fellowship, the nod of recognition from someone in the same community, someone who says to you what neither of us could ever prove to a third party: "we know." (173)

It is apparent here that because community in this sense is derived from consensus, it cannot become an object of study from outside the bounds of this assumed consensus. It is a theoretical construct signalled by the fact of agreement, the nod of recognition, and not a state of affairs, a set of social circumstances that can be examined to reveal anything significant about the nature of the agreements and the controversies it produces. Fish's earlier statement that interpretive strategies can themselves become the objects of dispute, although true, is inconsistent with this conception of community which depends on consensus.

This lack of explanatory power becomes clear when one asks how and why a particular paradigm or set of interpretive strategies is accepted or rejected by a community. Neither Kuhn nor Fish provides a satisfactory answer to this question. Much of Kuhn's description of a revolutionary period in the history of science is surprisingly similar to an objectivist account of hypothesis testing and falsification:

> Sometimes a normal problem, one that ought to be solvable by known rules and procedures, resists the reiterated onslought of the ablest members of the group within whose competence it falls. On other occasions a piece of equipment designed and constructed for the purpose of normal research fails to perform in the anticipated manner revealing an anomaly that cannot, despite repeated effort, be aligned with professional expectation. In these and other ways besides, normal science repeatedly goes astray. And when it does--when, that is, the profession can no longer evade anomalies that subvert the existing tradition of scientific practice--then begin the extraordinary investigations that lead the profession at last to a new set of commitments, a new basis for the practice of science. The extraordinary episodes in which that shift of professional commitments occurs are the ones known in this essay as scientific revolutions. (*The Structure of Scientific Revolutions*, 6)

and, "discovery commences with the awareness of anomaly, i.e., with the recognition that *nature has somehow violated the paradigm-induced expectations* that govern normal science" (52-53) (my emphasis). The reliance of this entire description on the idea of anomaly is problematic, not only because it is similar to the objectivist account, but also because there is little indication of what makes anomaly possible in the first place. Kuhn's account creates the impression that facts are bound to be compatible with theories within the framework of any paradigm, since they are constituted by those theories. It can be argued that since no paradigm is ever fully articulated in the stage in which it makes normal science possible, individual theories within paradigms can at any point prove insufficient to account for all the facts generated by the paradigm. But that certain facts, anomalous enough to lead to the discarding of the whole paradigm, can be observed and acknowledged by scientists who are still working under the assumptions of that paradigm seems to be contrary to Kuhn's notion that facts are theory-laden--since the anomalies, to be perceived as anomalies, must have broken free.

Fish provides an even more striking example of this problem while describing a Kuhnian revolution in linguistics. According to Fish, in the late sixties a group of Chomsky's best students challenged his model, which was the dominant linguistic paradigm at the time, by "pointing to data that could not be accommodated within [the model's] assumptions." In spite of the resistance of orthodox Chomskians,

> the weight of the unassimalable data proved too much for the model, and it more or less collapsed, taking with it much of the euphoria and optimism that had energized the field for a brief but glorious period. The workers in the field (or at least many of them) were in the position of no longer being able to believe in something they would have liked to believe in. (363)

Once again, paradigm change is explained by the resistance of facts to theories, and the community of researchers, instead of being the producer of facts, is said to be forced by them to abandon a position it had been socially and subjectively motivated to inhabit. This inconsistency supports my earlier observation that theories such as Fish's which seem to ascribe a determining role to communities--scientific, interpretive, or any other kind-- turn out to be quite incapable of using this concept in the analysis of crucial issues involving the production and the practical applications of knowledge. The inability to explain paradigm change is perhaps the most manifest symptom of not having a clear and functional concept of community, or of not having a way of defining paradigm and community independently of each other.

The same deficiency results in the fact that Fish's apparent transfer of authority and responsibility from impersonal notions such as truth and reality to communities does not have any practical consequences. Fish himself admits that his view that there are no facts about literary texts does not change anything in the practice of literary interpretation or education:

> The final question concerns the practical consequences of that argument. Since it is primarily a literary argument, one wonders what implications it has for the practice of literary criticism. The anwer is, none whatsoever. That is, it does not follow from what I have been saying that you should go out and do literary criticism in a certain way or refrain from doing it in other ways. The reason for this is that the position I have been presenting is not one that you (or anyone else) could live by. Its thesis is that whatever seems to you to be obvious and inescapable is only so within some institutional or conventional structure, and that means that you can never operate outside some such structure, even if you are persuaded by the thesis. As soon as you descend from theoretical reasoning about your assumptions, you will once again inhabit them and you will inhabit them without any reservations whatsoever. (370)

In other words, the critic is afflicted with a happy form of schizophrenia which enables him to advance in his profession in two disconnected ways. Even if his theoretical position denies the existence of objective, non-arbitrary textual facts, his membership in an interpretive community is complete and binding enough that the facts generated by that community's interpretive strategies seem to him, not only non-arbitrary, but also true and inescapable. In the meantime, his theoretical contributions to such questions as the nature of literary meaning, the objectivity of texts, etc. earn approval from the same community at conferences where the interpretation of individual texts is not the issue, but the legitimacy of literary criticism and education is.

Even though Fish is right in rejecting the assumption that "in order for something to be interesting, it must directly affect our every day experience of poetry" (370-71), his rigid distinction between criticism and meta-criticism or theory is still questionable. By raising the issue of the relationship between his theory and the practice of literary criticism and then reducing this issue to the question of the critic's belief in her current interpretation of a text, Fish is actually displaying the same attitude that he criticizes as being "anti-theoretical" and "parochial." That is, by using phrases such as "practical consequences" and "the practice of literary criticism" interchangably with "practical criticism," he is accepting the assumption that the only possible practical consequences of a literary theory have to be sought at the level of interpretation. If we follow Fish's lead and look for those consequences in the framework of a critic's faith in her own interpretations of texts, we will be likely to agree with him that there are indeed no such consequences, since "while relativism is a position one can entertain, it is not a position one can occupy" (319).

Whatever his beliefs about the determinacy or objectivity of meaning, a critic cannot choose not to believe in his own interpretation of a text.

But although Fish assures us that what he develops is "primarily a literary argument," a theory like his, if it took its own emphasis on community seriously, would have consequences beyond the question of interpretation. It would have to address such issues as established literary canons, the methods and purposes of teaching literature, the nature of aesthetic pleasure, and the like with a new perspective. Since it claims that these issues cannot be decided by reference to objective standards existing independently of communal decisions, it would have to investigate and perhaps offer alternatives to the processes through which those decisions are made.

Fish's willingness to bypass these issues for the most part and use his model of interpretive communities to emphasize consensus rather than controversy, authority rather than the challenges against it, is not an inevitable consequence of his epistemological principles or his reader-based approach to literature. The same positions are often being defended as theoretical bases for radical critiques of established literary institutions. In any case, I do not find it useful to revive the well-known objections that have been made to relativism on political grounds. I am willing to grant Fish's point that "while it is generally true that to have many standards is to have none at all, it is not true for anyone in particular . . . and therefore is a truth of which one can say 'it doesn't matter'" (319). The purpose of my critique has been to illustrate the *methodological* inadequacies of a critical approach that employs the concept of community as primarily an epistemological category. Fish appeals to the communal nature of interpretation in order to prevent his rejection of textual facts from leading to an intellectual anarchism according to which "anything goes." Since he avoids replacing textual facts with sociological ones even though in principle he seems to require them (Oscar Kenshur, "The Rhetoric of Incommensurability," 379), he cannot make community itself the object of his analysis. Whatever the merits of his theory in other respects, the circularities inherent in his definitions of community prevent him from providing a framework for seeing literary texts and their interpretations as truly social phenomena.

CHAPTER 6

CONCLUSION

Louis Althusser, Jacques Derrida, and Stanley Fish represent three very different approaches to the social contexts of discourse. Althusser's theory of ideology is an explicitly political theory which defines ideology by its function of perpetuating existing relations of domination and exploitation in a society. Derrida's more abstract, philosophical deconstruction of what he calls metaphysics aims to question the authority of all universal claims, but because it connects metaphysical systems of thought to repressive institutions on the one hand and to the exclusion of the "others" of Western society on the other hand, it is seen as having political consquences by most deconstructionists and by Derrida himself. And Fish's obviously apolitical theory of interpretive communities nevertheless seems to place interpretation in a social context by grounding both the possibility and the validity of interpretations on the notion of community.

On the basis of this initial account, one would expect each of these three theories to lead to different strategies for studying language and literature from the viewpoint of their involvement in particular social conflicts. One would expect to learn from Althusser how to identify the relationships between different types of domination and the ideas, practices, and institutions which legitimate them; from Derrida, how to invalidate the universal and absolute claims of metaphysics by revealing the particular realities and contradictions which they conceal; and from Fish, how to identify the community interests which authorize certain interpretive strategies and exclude others. These insights should in turn provide criteria for determining the conflicting purposes which literary texts as well as other forms of public discourse serve, both in their production and reception.

However, when we examine the overall theoretical frameworks which Althusser, Derrida, and Fish offer, we find that their key terms, ideology, metaphysics, and community, are not very useful for discriminating between such conflicting purposes. These terms are abstract and ambiguous because they are used to account for too many things at once. In the case of Althusser, ideology is both a political category and an epistemological one. In political terms, it is defined by a social function. As an epistemological category, it mediates between consciousness and reality, and it is used to dissolve the empiricist opposition between subjects and the object world. Something very similar is true of Fish's theory. Community is both a sociological category and an epistemological one. On the one hand, it seems to refer to particular social groups and institutions; on the other hand, it is used as a theoretical hypothesis to reject all the distinctions between subjective and objective facts, literal and interpretive meanings, while still avoiding anarchy and solipsism. Derrida also uses his basic term, metaphysics, in at least two senses, or rather two different levels of generality. On the one hand, metaphysics is both a philosophical and an ideological term. It denotes systems of thought which are built on false claims to absolute truth, pure presence, universal authority, etc., and which rationalize social domination and institutional authority. On the other hand, metaphysics is the structure of all language and thought, the only means we have of knowledge, communication, and interpretation, at least in the Western world.

The fundamental ambiguities of these three terms, their complexly interrelated but also problematic definitions on political, sociological, and epistemological levels, constitute both their strength and their weakness. That it is a strength is easily proven by the frustrating experience of trying to argue with these writers, especially with Derrida and Fish. The shifting meanings of metaphysics and community give them a great deal of polemical flexibility. However, my analysis of each of these terms from the viewpoint of its usefulness for ideological or sociological criticism indicates that this ambiguity is also a weakness. These terms often turn out to be either too inclusive or too restrictive to account for the phenomena that matter most for political analyses: change, conflict, disagreement, differences in degrees of autonomy, degrees of authority, etc.

For example, when Fish uses the term interpretive community to refer to the narrowly defined academic institution, that is, when he uses the term in a sociological way, he cannot account for the changes and the radical disagreements that often occur within that institution. He simply has to assume that all those changes and disagreements had actually been authorized by the variety of available interpretive strategies, but that is just a way of assuming what one had aimed to explain in the first place.

On the other hand, when he uses the term in the more general, epistemological sense of intersubjectivity, of what makes any agreement possible, when he says that the existence of an interpretive community is signalled by the fact of agreement, this community can neither become an object of knowledge nor serve the purpose Fish wants it toserve, namely, preventing intellectual anarchy. Community in this sense is as homogenous and subjective as an individual. According to this logic, every disagreement within a community should result in its splitting into smaller communities, and this process would simply bring back the anarchy the notion of community was supposed to avoid.

Althusser's general epistemological definition of ideology as a mediator between subject and object, as the process of the constitution of the subject, when interpreted by itself, becomes quite irrelevant to political issues. It is simply equivalent to all conscious life. On the other hand, it becomes too restrictive and leads to problems when taken together with his political definition of ideology by its function of preserving existing relations of domination. If all subjects are constituted as subjects through a process that insures the continuance of existing social relations, we cannot explain the presence of alternative political viewpoints or the possibility of a critique of ideology, "scientific" or otherwise.

When Derrida defines metaphysics as a philosophy of absolute and immediate truth, of divine authority, universal hierarchization, etc., his deconstruction of it is convincing, but not as scandalous and new as his rhetoric makes it seem. Metaphysics in this sense is a particular philosophical tradition which has had its challengers throughout the history of philosophy. More importantly, when this definition of metaphysics is used as the basis of an ideological critique, it is too restrictive because it does not apply to the cases in which relations of domination are supported and rationalized by "non-metaphysical" views such as relativism or scepticism. In the sense in which these views can also be shown to be metaphysical, in the sense in which all categories of thought are based on distinctions and assumptions which are ultimately metaphysical, this term becomes too inclusive. The deconstruction of metaphysics defined in this way inevitably takes the form of working concepts to a kind of exhaustion to reveal their epistemological impurities. This form of deconstruction can be thought of as a method rather than a theory, and it might be useful for specific purposes in specific contexts. However, its value is limited because the impurities of concepts do not automatically invalidate them, and there is nothing in the nature of deconstruction that indicates under what circumstances a concept becomes "too metaphysical" to retain, and under what circumstances it can still be used, in spite of its impurities.

Althusserian and deconstructionist valorizations of literary discourse, Derrida's treatment of the notion of subjecthood and his conception of "femininity," and Fish's failure to make his theory relevant to the practice of literary criticism or to a sociological understanding of literary institutions are all examples of how such overinclusive and ambiguous categories lead to abstract and acontextual analyses. "Literature" deconstructs metaphysics, or dismantles ideology, but all this happens quite independently of the circumstances under which literary texts are produced and interpreted. Similarly, the metaphysical notion of the subject is countered with such abstract notions as "decenteredness" or "femininity" without taking account of the different historical and political contexts in which subjecthood has been defined. In the case of Fish, the notion of community is used to assert that interpretation always takes place in a context, but it does not tell us anything about actual communities and actual contexts.

We can conclude from these observations that the social aspects of literature and other types of discourse cannot be defined through "master categories" like "ideology" and "community" which are at the same time epistemological terms used to explain the mechanisms of meaning and perception in general, or a category like "metaphysics," which is at the same time a philosophical term used to cast doubt on the very possibility of meaning and perception in general. What is needed is an avoidance of "theory" in this sense rather than a new theory which is based on a new master category.

The categories for an ideological analysis of literary texts are provided not by general theories of meaning, language, and consciousness, but by the social contexts in which these texts are written and read. Accordingly, any type of criticism which aims to view literature as a social phenomenon must start from an investigation of those contexts. Such an investigation requires not a general method of demystification, but a social analysis by the aid of which the critic can define the nature of the specific values and representations to be criticized, and the alternative values and representations which make this criticism possible. On the basis of such an analysis, both literary texts and literary institutions can be examined in relation to real social conflicts without being locked into abstract generalizations or self-refuting relativisms. Feminist criticism, to the extent to which it takes real social conflicts as a point of departure and posits itself as an element in those conflicts, provides a good example of such a critical practice.

WORKS CITED

Adorno, Theodor and Max Horkheimer. *The Dialectics of Enlightenment.* New York: Herder and Herder, 1972.
Althusser, Louis. "Freud and Lacan." *In Lenin and Philosophy.* New York and London: Monthly Review Press, 1972.
----------. "Ideology and Ideological State Apparatuses." In *Lenin and Philosophy.* New York and London: Monthly Review Press, 1972.
----------. *Lenin and Philosophy.* Trans. Ben Brewster. New York and London: Monthly Review Press, 1972.
Arac, Jonathan, ed. *Postmodernism and Politics.* Minneapolis: University of Minnesota Press, 1986.
Altieri, Charles. "Wittgenstein on Consciousness and Language: A Challenge to Derridean Literary Theory." *MLN* 91 (1976): 1397-1423.
Aronowitz, Stanley. *The Crisis of Historical Materialism: Class, Politics, and Culture in Marxist Theory.* New York: Praeger, 1981.
Baker, Francis. *The Tremulous Private Body: Essays on Subjection.* London: Methuen, 1984.
Barthes, Roland. *Critical Essays.* Evanston: Northwestern University Press, 1972.
----------. *Image-Music-Text.* Trans. Stephen Heath. New York: Hill and Wang, 1977.
----------. *The Pleasure of the Text.* New York: Hill and Wang, 1974.
Baxandull, Lee and Stefan Morawski ed. *Marx and Engels on Artand Literature.* Milwaukee: Telos Press, 1973.
Beauvoir, Simone. *The Second Sex.* New York: Knopf, 1953.
Bloom, Harold, et al. *Deconstruction and Criticism.* New York: Seabury, 1979.
Bové, Paul, et al. *The Question of Textuality: Strategies of Reading in Contemporary American Criticism.* Bloomington: Indiana University Press, 1982.
Culler, Jonathan. *On Deconstruction: Theory and Criticism After Structuralism.* New York: Cornell University Press, 1982.
Davis, Robert Con and Ronald Schleifer ed. *Rhetoric and Form: Deconstruction at Yale.* Norman: University of Oklahoma Press, 1985.
De Man, Paul. *Allegories of Reading: Figural Language in Rousseau, Nietzsche, Rilke and Proust.* New Haven: Yale University Press, 1979.
----------. *Blindness and Insight: Essays in the Rhetoric of Contemporary Criticism.* New York: Oxford University Press, 1971.

----------. *The Resistance to Theory*. Minneapolis: University of Minnesota Press, 1986.

----------. "The Task of the Translator." In *Resistance toTheory*. Minneapolis: University of Minnesota Press, 1986.

Derrida, Jacques. "But Beyond. . .(Open Letter to Ann McClintok and Rob Nixon." *Critical Inquiry* 13 (Autumn1986): 155-70.

----------. "Choreographies: Interview with Christie V. McDonald." *Diacritics* 12 (Summer 1982): 66-76.

----------. "Differance." In *Speech and Phenomena*. Evanston: Northwestern University Press, 1973.

----------. "The Ends of Man." In *The Margins of Philosophy*. Chicago: University of Chicago Press, 1983.

----------. "Living On: Border Lines." In *Deconstruction and Criticism*. New York: Seabury, 1979.

----------. *The Margins of Philosophy*. Chicago: University of Chicago Press, 1983.

----------. *Of Grammatology*. Trans. Gayatri Chakravorty Spivak. Baltimore and London: Johns Hopkins University Press, 1976.

----------. *Positions*. Trans. Alan Bass. Chicago: University of Chicago Press, 1981.

----------. "Sending: On Representation." *Social Research* 49 (Summer 1982): 294-326.

----------. *Spurs: Nietzsche's Styles*. Trans. Barbara Harlow. Chicago: University of Chicago Press, 1979.

----------. "Structure, Sign, and Play." In *Writing and Difference*. Trans. Alan Bass. Chicago: University of Chicago Press, 1978.

----------. *Writing and Difference*. Trans. Alan Bass. Chicago: University of Chicago Press, 1978.

Eagleton, Terry. *Marxism and Literary Criticism*. London: Methuen Books, 1976.

Fish, Stanley. *Is There A Text In This Class?: The Authority of Interpretive Communities*. Cambridge: Harvard University Press, 1982.

Frazer, Nancy. "The French Derridians: Politicizing Deconstruction or Deconstructing the Political." *New German Critique* 18 (1983): 127-54.

Graff, Gerald. *Poetic Statement and Critical Dogma*. Evanston: Northwestern University Press, 1970.

----------. "The Pseudo-Politics of Interpretation." In *The Politics of Interpretation*. Ed. W. J. T. Mitchell. Chicago: University of Chicago Press, 1983.

Handelman, Susan. *The Slayers of Moses: the Emergence of Rabbinic Interpretation in Modern Literary Theory*. Albany, New York: State University of New York, 1982.

Hartman, Geoffrey. *Criticism in the Wilderness: The Study of Literature Today*. New Haven: Yale University Press, 1980.

Higgins, John. "Raymond Williams and the Problem of Ideology." In *Postmodernism and Politics*. Jonathan Arac ed. Minneapolis: University of Minnesota Press, 1986.

Hirst, Paul. "Althusser and the Theory of Ideology." *Economy and Society* 5 (1976): 385-412.

Irigeray, Luce. *The Speculum of the Other Woman*. Trans. Gillian G. Gill. Ithaca, New York: Cornell University Press, 1985.

Johnson, Barbara. *The Critical Difference: Essays in The Contemporary Rhetoric of Reading*. Baltimore: Johns Hopkins University Press, 1980.

Kenshur, Oscar. "Demystifying the Demystifiers: Metaphysical Snares of Ideological Criticism." *Critical Inquiry* 14 (Winter, 1988): 335-53.

----------. "The Rhetoric of Incommensurability." *JAAC* XLII (Summer 1984): 375-81.

Knapp, Steven, and Walter Benn Michaels. "Against Theory 2: Hermeneutics and Deconstruction." *Critical Inquiry* 14 (Autumn 1987): 49-68.

Kristeva, Julia. *Desire in Language*. New York: Columbia University Press, 1980.

Krupnik, Mark, ed. *Displacement: Derrida and After*. Bloomington and London: Indiana University Press, 1983.

Kuhn, Thomas. *The Essential Tension: Selected Studies in Scientific Tradition and Change*. Chicago: University of Chicago Press, 1977.

----------. *The Structure of Scientific Revolutions*. Chicago: University of Chicago Press, 1962.

Lauretis, Teresa de. *Alice Doesn't: Feminism, Semiotics, Cinema*. Bloomington: Indiana University Press, 1984.

----------, ed. *Feminist Studies/Critical Studies*. Bloomington: Indiana University Press, 1986.

Lentricchia, Frank. *After the New Criticism*. Chicago: University of Chicago Press, 1980.

Levi-Strauss, Claude. *The Raw and the Cooked*. Trans. John and Doreen Wightman. New York: Harper and Row, 1969.

Macherey, Pierre. *A Theory of Literary Production*. Trans. Geoffrey Wall. London: Verso, 1978.

Marx, Karl and Frederick Engels. *German Ideology*. New York: International Publishers, 1947.

Miller, Hillis. "Critic As Host." In *Deconstruction and Criticism*. New York: Seabury, 1979.

----------. "Deconstructing the Deconstructors." *Diacritics* 5:2 (1975): 24-31.

Mitchell, W. J. T., ed. *The Politics of Interpretation*. Chicago: University of Chicago Press, 1983.

Modleski, Tania. "Feminism and the Power of Interpretation." In *Feminist Studies/Critical Studies*. Teresa de Lauretis ed. Bloomington: Indiana University Press, 1986.

Nietzsche, Frederick. *The Gay Science*. Trans. Walter J.Kaufmann. New York: Vintage Books, 1974.

Norris, Christopher. "Some Versions of Rhetoric: Empson and De Man." In *Rhetoric and Form: Deconstruction at Yale*. Robert Con Davis and Ronald Schleifer ed. Norman: University of Oklahoma Press, 1985.

Popper, Karl. *The Open Society and Its Enemies*. Princeton, N.J.: Princeton University Press, 1963.

Rorty, Richard. "Deconstruction and Circumvention." *Critical Inquiry* 11 (Fall 1984): 1-23.

----------. "Nineteenth-Century Idealism and Twentieth-Century Textualism." *Monist* 64 (1981): 155-74.

Ryan, Michael. *Marxism and Deconstruction: A Critical Articulation*. Baltimore: Johns Hopkins University Press, 1982.

Said, Edward. "Opponents, Audiences, Constituencies, and Community." *Critical Inquiry* (Fall 1982): 178-96.

Saussure, Ferdinand. *Course in General Linguistics*. NewYork: McGraw-Hill, 1966.

Scholes, Robert. "Deconstruction and Communication." *Critical Inquiry* 14 (Winter 1988), 278-95.

----------. *Textual Power: Literary Theory and the Teaching of English*. New Haven: Yale University Press, 1985.

Searle, John. "Reiterating the Differences: A Reply to Derrida." *Glyph* I (1977): 198-208.

Spivak, Gayatri Chakravorty. "Displacement and the Discourse of Woman." In *Displacement*. Mark Krupnik ed. Bloomington and London: Indiana University Press, 1983.

----------. "The Politics of Interpretations." *Critical Inquiry* (Fall 1982): 259-78.

Thompson, John B. *Studies in the Theory of Ideology*. Berkeley: University of California Press, 1984.

Watkins, Evan. "The Politics of Literary Criticism." In *The Question of Textuality*. Ed. Paul Bové et al. Bloomington: Indiana University Press, 1982.

Williams, Raymond. *Writing in Society*. London: Verso, 1984.

For Product Safety Concerns and Information please contact our EU representative GPSR@taylorandfrancis.com
Taylor & Francis Verlag GmbH, Kaufingerstraße 24, 80331 München, Germany

www.ingramcontent.com/pod-product-compliance
Lightning Source LLC
Chambersburg PA
CBHW070404240426
43661CB00056B/2529